Spirituality of

# GRATITUDE

The Unexpected Blessings of Thankfulness

JOSHUA CHOONMIN KANG

IVP Books

An imprint of InterVarsity Press
Downers Grove, Illinois

InterVarsity Press
P.O. Box 1400, Downers Grove, IL 60515-1426
ivpress.com
email@ivpress.com

InterVarsity Press® is the book-publishing division of InterVarsity Christian Fellowship/USA®, a movement of students and faculty active on campus at hundreds of universities, colleges and schools of nursing in the United States of America, and a member movement of the International Fellowship of Evangelical Students. For information about local and regional activities, visit intervarsity.org.

While any stories in this book are true, some names and identifying information may have been changed to protect the privacy of individuals.

Cover design: Cindy Kiple
Interior design: Beth McGill

Images: One of a series of birds and fruit paintings by Wang Guochen at School of Oriental & African Studies Library, University of London, Bridgeman Images.

ISBN 978-0-8308-4603-0 (print)
ISBN 978-0-8308-9859-6 (digital)

Printed in the United States of America ♾

 As a member of the Green Press Initiative, InterVarsity Press is committed to protecting the environment and to the responsible use of natural resources. To learn more, visit greenpressinitiative.org.

**Library of Congress Cataloging-in-Publication Data**

Kang, Joshua Choonmin.
  Spirituality of gratitude : the unexpected blessings of thankfulness / Joshua Choonmin Kang.
    pages cm
  Includes bibliographical references.
  ISBN 978-0-8308-4603-0 (pbk. : alk. paper)
  1. Gratitude—Religious aspects—Christianity. 2. Spiritual life—Christianity. I. Title.
  BV4647.G8K36 2015
  241'.4—dc23
                                    2015013542

| P | 20 | 19 | 18 | 17 | 16 | 15 | 14 | 13 | 12 | 11 | 10 | 9 | 8 | 7 | 6 | 5 | 4 | 3 | 2 | 1 |
| Y | 32 | 31 | 30 | 29 | 28 | 27 | 26 | 25 | 24 | 23 | 22 | 21 | 20 | 19 | 18 | 17 | 16 | 15 |

# Contents

# 1

# An Invitation to the Spirituality of Gratitude

*D*eep gratitude springs up from within. To become *truly* grateful is incredibly difficult, but the difficulty of the process makes the results all the more lovely.

I recently experienced a very difficult season of life. I felt helpless and hopeless, weakened and powerless from all that was happening. I had not been blind to my own frailty, but it was during those days that I realized what a finite being I truly am. Yet throughout, I yearned for gratitude. I wanted to be grateful and for that gratitude to sustain me.

Now, I am not talking about being excited by the tragedies that befall us. It is extremely difficult, if not impossible, to be thankful for hardship or tragedy or pain during a crisis. How can a person diagnosed with cancer be grateful for the cancer? How can one be thankful for losing a loved one in a tragic accident? If anyone knows gratitude in that circumstance it is not for the crisis itself, but for God's sovereignty *in the midst of* suffering. We know that God would not allow a tragedy to happen to us for the purpose of revealing his sovereignty, but his sovereignty can *transform* a tragedy. Whatever is lifted up to God can be made beautiful.

The Scriptures teach that "God is love" and that God loves sovereignly; he knows everything in his love. The only thing *we* can do is be grateful for who he is and what he has done. But it is only when we trust God's sovereign love that we can be thankful for all things (Romans 8:28). So our gratitude is founded on God's character. Colossians 2:7 reminds us of this truth, for when we are deeply *rooted* in Jesus Christ we overflow with gratitude.

Roots define the future of the tree. In order to harvest abundant, good fruit one must take good care of a tree's roots. But the signs of a dying tree can be easily missed, and unless a person is a tree expert, root disease is not always diagnosed. Infected leaves—the evidence of disease—can be pruned, but that alone is not the cure. If the root system is not addressed, the tree will die.

Grumbling and blaming are the fruit of the sick roots in our hearts, and the evidence of decay is revealed in our words. The call to gratitude is the invitation to a life of tending and guarding the inner gardens of our hearts, remembering that "the mouth speaks what the heart is full of" (Matthew 12:34). Whether we are thankful does not depend on our circumstances, but on our hearts.

Gratitude heals us and holds us, tethering us to one another, offering us joy and strength. So let us enter deeply into the world of gratitude. Let us walk together on this journey of thanksgiving. Let us experience our sovereign God, to whom we give thanks forever. And let us learn gratitude and the language of thanksgiving as we journey on.

Part One

## A Source of Grace

# 2

# The Grace of Endurance

One of God's graces is the grace of endurance. There is a close relationship between endurance and gratitude, for the strength to endure suffering comes from gratitude.

Job received the grace of endurance. He endured as much hardship as a person could ever experience, losing his children, his wealth and his health, suffering criticism and blame from those closest to him. And God's silence in the midst of suffering multiplied his pain. But Job endured. Although God remained silent, we know that he was *with* Job and Job endured faithfully.

We often face hardships we can't endure on our own and need patience to abide. Like passing through a long tunnel, we have no choice but to be patient until we reach the end.

The length of endurance defines the length of the usage. A tree that endures the seasons will be useful. As a master carpenter, Tsunekazu Nishioka knows this to be true. His family has taken care of Hōryū-ji, a Buddhist temple and one of the world's oldest wooden structures, for over 1,400 years.

Nishioka asserts that "in order to build a structure that will last for one thousand years, one must use the timbers that have endured for longer than one thousand years." The length of endurance defines the length of usage.

In order to endure well, we need the power of acceptance. No one enjoys suffering. However, if the suffering is somehow embraced, then it can become a precious treasure. We can learn about the importance of endurance from the oyster. An intruder slips into the shell and irritates it. The shell embraces the intruder and produces nacre, a strong, resilient material, to coat it layer by layer, resulting in a pearl. Thus, the oyster's endurance produces a pearl.

It is gratitude that can transform our sufferings into blessings. Sufferings invite pain, but if we befriend the sufferings and consider them learning opportunities, they lose their power in our lives and can result in a thing of beauty.

When we give thanks, we become more able to accept our circumstances, even our suffering and pain. So joy or even miracles can come to us through acceptance. Many miracles in the Bible happened to those who embraced their problems and brought them to God. To deny our suffering is to miss the experience of God's miracles in our lives.

Jesus embraced difficulties, sympathizing with those who brought their problems to him. He had compassion on hurting people, often confronting their obstacles as opportunities. And Jesus prayed the prayer of thanksgiving *in the midst of* difficulties. This kind of gratitude allows us to embrace our problems and make room for God's miracles.

The strength of endurance defines the depth of beauty. When ceramics have endured the burning furnace, they come out beautiful. And the higher the furnace temperature, the more beautiful the vessels become. But only those vessels that have gone through the fire maintain their beautiful color and shape over the course of time.

Endurance is closely linked to usefulness, for the biblical figures used by God's hand endured hardships. They endured in the pit, the prison, the wilderness, the cave, the fiery furnace and the lion's den. But they were people of gratitude who received and enjoyed God's grace to endure and to be used by him.

When we are facing hardships and the inevitable sufferings of life, we can be grateful for our situation and endure with faith, trusting that there will be a time to be used by God in a mighty way. Enduring with perseverance allows us to enjoy God's grace, and endurance will enable us to serve his kingdom better.

# 3

# The Grace of Descending

*T*rue gratitude is being grateful for everything. Being thankful for a wonderful situation is easy. But true gratitude is being thankful for the situation we can't be thankful for by our own strength. That kind of gratitude can be found only by one who knows the paradox of grace.

One paradox of grace is gratitude for "descending." We honor and applaud those who ascend—those who have earned achievement or success. On the other hand, we often pity, avoid or even scorn those who descend.

Those who have reached the pinnacle of success have ascended to the summit, and the summit can be a precious place. Some things can *only* be seen from that vantage point. There is much to learn from those who have reached the heights, and they can serve as excellent guides to lead others. But the summit can also be a dangerous place of exposure and vulnerability. It is not a good place for a long stay, and everyone who has ascended must eventually descend. But this can be a painful and terribly lonely experience, even more dangerous than the ascent.

Timing is key to a proper descent. When Peter Hillary, the son of world-famous mountain climber Sir Edmund Hillary, conquered Mount Everest in 2002, he called his father from atop the mountain. His father's advice was to "be more careful when you come down from that mountain. It is much harder to come down from the mountain than climbing up the mountain." One can get lost or fall, even die, on the down side of the mountain if the proper timing is missed. But only those who have reached the summit know how it feels to descend.

We need God's grace in order to conquer the summit. But coming down requires just as much of God's grace. Think of an airplane. If the airplane descends carefully and safely, we call it "landing." However, if the airplane loses control during the descent, as the result of turbulence or other outside forces, we call it "crashing." Likewise, if a person who has reached the leadership summit descends willingly, it is considered to be beautiful. On the other hand, if a leader is forcibly removed from the summit, it can be a humiliating downfall. We need God's special grace in order to make a beautiful descent.

Leaders who descend beautifully, in God's perfect timing, can experience his amazing grace like never before. There may be new opportunities for them as a result of descending well at the proper time, having even greater impact in a new endeavor. When we descend, we are offered a different view. "The Flower of the Moment," a poem by Nobel Prize–nominated poet Ko Un, describes this concept:

*On the way down, I saw the flower I hadn't seen on the way up.*

Let us be thankful on the way down, for God's hidden grace is at the bottom, and it is there that we understand hardship.

There's unexplainable depth at the bottom that simply can't be felt at the top, which is why those used by God's hand all experience severe hardships. And if we allow the rock-bottom experience to refine and redefine us, we can protect ourselves from falling from the top. Jesus' cross is that low place, but that cross reaches to heaven. This is why I daily draw near to the low place of the cross.

# 4

# The Grace of Isolation

*G*ratitude is mysterious and marvelous. The mystery of gratitude is that some people can give thanks in impossible circumstances—thanksgiving in the midst of isolation.

Isolation is the state of being locked in. Joseph was pushed into a cistern by his own brothers, which led to eleven years of isolation in Potiphar's house, followed by another two years in jail. Joseph was completely isolated from the outside world for many years. But God graciously transformed Joseph's isolated days into blessed days. God's favor meant that those years were not wasted. Instead, Joseph dreamed dreams and prepared for his future, gaining the necessary knowledge to become a political leader.

When God prepares someone for leadership, he often allows that person to experience isolation. Isolation is lonely and sad, leaving us feeling abandoned and misunderstood. Surrounded by enemies and opposition, it can be a painful time of brokenness, betrayal and destruction. Worse yet, we often feel forgotten.

Moses experienced isolation for forty years in the wilderness. David was also isolated in the wilderness, in the cave of Abdullam and in Palestine, confessing in the Psalms that he was in "the miry pit." The prophet Jeremiah was confined and imprisoned many times, even left to die in a cistern of mud. The apostle Paul spent three years of isolation in the desert area in Arabia, and a long time imprisoned in Rome during the peak of his life. These were painful seasons, but God didn't waste this pain. Those days became precious because of gratitude. Paul's prison epistles are filled with gratitude, crying out, "Rejoice always . . . give thanks in all circumstances" (1 Thessalonians 5:16, 18). Gratitude has a mysterious power, enabling us to be content no matter where we are and to recognize God's sovereignty and will.

The secret to the victorious life lies in finding contentment where we are. Mother Teresa said, "love the place where you stay even more." Joseph was content wherever he was. He served there, and he learned there, and prepared for his future there. It's not that Joseph didn't experience suffering, but he knew contentment because of his trust in the Lord, who was with him.

When we experience gratitude during a period of isolation, the time of isolation can become a time of blessing. During the winter season, trees stop all activities on the surface. Though barren, the winter tree maintains its roots. It saves energy to blossom when the spring comes. It is the same with God's people. We need, sometimes, to stop external activities and go through an isolated time. Only then can we look after our interior world, to reflect and grow deeper.

Many people experience deep growth during their time of isolation. John Bunyan wrote *The Pilgrim's Progress* in prison.

Nelson Mandela created great unity and lived a wonderful life in a terrible prison for twenty-seven years. When Hudson Taylor became sick and lived for five years like a hermit, he started the China Inland Mission.

We can be grateful for the grace of God-given isolation, forgiving and blessing those who isolated us. In God's perfect time, he will rescue us from the unexplainable cistern. But even when it is difficult, let us love the places where we are planted. Let us serve where we are and love those we meet. Although people may forget us, God never forgets us.

# 5

# The Grace of Humility

*T*o be grateful is to discover, so we need to open our eyes to find something for which we can be grateful. Even the ability to be grateful has nothing to do with our own effort; it is the result of God's grace. When our eyes are open, we become thankful for things we might not otherwise appreciate and for things we previously took for granted.

When we experience God's grace, our perspective is changed, and we are able to recognize the good in the ordinary. We see the good side of the people we meet, and the light in the midst of darkness. We learn to appreciate any kind of person and any circumstance, often being impressed and touched by nearly everything around us. When that happens, we notice God's love in every situation. We become grateful for everything we enjoy, seeing how undeserving we are.

But this kind of gratitude can only be found in the humble heart. God wants us to become humble because he wants to bestow his grace on us from the lowly place. It is there that we kneel down and even fall on our faces before him in our times of suffering. But it is also there that we experience his amazing grace, for his *greatest* grace is found at the *lowest* place.

When we notice people of authority who serve others humbly, our hearts are touched. We learn from them that our rank or position is not what matters, but our attitude. We know that there is nothing we can take with us when we leave this earth, and what makes us long for eternity has nothing to do with our station in life. There is a deeper joy that resides within our hearts. What is precious is invisible and untouchable, and it is often met in the low places.

Jesus came to a low place. Jesus, exalted as the highest King, was the utmost example of humility. Humility brings peace, for when we reach the low place, we needn't worry about falling down anymore. Those in high places are anxious to protect their position, but those in low places have nothing to protect and no need to battle for supremacy. God's *shalom*, the best grace that his people pursue, is found in the low places.

Temptations and tests always seduce us from the top. Whatever we gain and enjoy at the heights will ultimately end. Popularity, wealth, glory and power are fleeting, and what we don't willingly relinquish will be taken away. We may resent loss if things are taken from us, but we can experience satisfaction if we give them away first.

Joy is found at the low places and in small things. When we see God's smile in a child's smiling face, our lives are not in vain. When we share a crust of bread with a neighbor, we understand the true meaning of life. When we wonder at the mystery of the universe while gazing at a wildflower, we are blessed. Seeking the high places and the best things distracts us from pure and simple pleasures for which we can be grateful.

# 6

# The Grace of Brokenness

*W*e also experience God's grace through brokenness. Brokenness is a reflection of sufferings and sorrow; it is painful, often leaving scars. It is paradoxical that gratitude often comes through brokenness, and yet there is a grace that the broken one can still be offered to God.

It is a great mystery that brokenness garners wisdom and understanding. The experience of comfort does not offer the same depth wrought by hardship.

Our generation seems quite satisfied with shallow grace, a "light" generation. Sufferings are scorned, and depth is dismissed. But the word *glory* in Hebrew means "weight" or "heaviness." There is *weight* to God's glory. Paul said, "Oh, the depth of the riches of the wisdom and knowledge of God! How unsearchable his judgments, and his paths beyond tracing out!" (Romans 11:33). Worldly wisdom is shallow, but God's wisdom and knowledge are deep.

God favors holy depth over shallow knowledge, and holy depth comes through brokenness. When a grain of wheat is buried in the ground and dead, it bears many fruits (John 12:24). Being buried and dead is another way of describing the process of brokenness. The life of a plant lies in the seed, but life only emerges when the seed breaks. Without brokenness, there's no root; without roots, there can be no fragrant flowers or abundant fruit.

Jesus allowed himself to be broken on the cross as he gave his own flesh and blood for us. Henri Nouwen once said that unless something is broken, it can't be shared. At the Last Supper, Jesus took the bread, broke it and shared it with the disciples. To love is to break something precious *for* the one who is loved. Thus the communion table is the table of brokenness.

The woman who broke the alabaster jar took the most precious thing she had and broke it for Jesus, anointing him with her love as he faced the cross alone. But the fragrance was not experienced until the jar was broken. So we find that from brokenness life flows out and the fragrance can be enjoyed.

What I mean by brokenness is *complete* brokenness, shattered to the point of becoming powder. In the Old Testament, grain offerings were broken into bits (Leviticus 6:21). In order to be used by God, one must be broken and crumbled first like the grain offering of flour.

Through brokenness, the potential within us is revealed. In order for a plant to grow, the kernel of the seed—but not the entire seed—must break. Our brokenness offers understanding that we can use in helping others. God uses our brokenness for his glory.

We don't need to fear brokenness. Instead, we can be thankful for it, for through it we grow in depth and maturity.

Part Two

# What We Are Grateful For

# 7

# Problems

*I* am filled with gratitude for my problems. As I study the Scriptures, I realize that where there were problems, there were also God's miracles. In fact, problems and troubles were the necessary foundation for God's miracles. No one enjoys trouble, since one problem seems to lead to another. We desire peace and safety; problems shake our foundation and make us insecure. But if there is no problem, there is no miracle. We need the right perspective to approach and respond to a problem, or rather, we need *God's* perspective on the problems we face. That is wisdom.

Our growth carries the residue of our challenges, so problems become essential to our maturity. In fact, we often grow in direct proportion to the number and severity of our problems. For a long time I feared problems, attempting to avoid them, which only caused me to stumble more. But when I decided to confront them I realized that they are opportunities for God to perform his great work.

We all face problems in life. When Jesus was faced with

problems, he began with thanksgiving. Before feeding thousands of hungry people with five loaves and two fish, he offered a prayer of thanks. Before calling Lazarus from his tomb, Jesus offered thanks. In the presence of thanksgiving, our problems lose their power because they are confronted by Jesus. He endured the cross to solve the horrible problem of sin in our lives.

In this way, gratitude affords the opportunity for problems to become treasures. So we need not be afraid of the problems when they come to us, for God often wraps his blessings in problems. When we refuse to face our problems, we might just be rejecting God's gifts.

So we can treat our problems carefully, unraveling them as one might unwind a bobbin. Then we can take those problems to our Father in prayer, giving thanks in all circumstances (1 Thessalonians 5:18). When we are able to have God's perspective on the problems and troubles of our lives, then we are able to experience his blessing and even his miracles, gaining wisdom and growing in maturity.

Whatever the problems we are facing, let us give thanksgiving to the Lord for them, trusting that each will be an opportunity to know him more and enjoy his blessing.

# 8

# Thorns

*T*here can be gratitude for "thorns in the flesh." Thorns inflict pain and bring tears. Paul had a thorn in the flesh that weakened him. Although Paul pleaded for the thorn to be removed—for healing—God's answer was, "My grace is sufficient for you." The thorn served to remind Paul of his weaknesses and his dependence on Christ.

Sometimes the painful poking of a thorn reminds us that we are still alive. A person with Hansen's disease, also known as leprosy, cannot feel pain. Once Paul Brand, a famous leprosy doctor, asked one of his patients what would be the greatest gift that he could receive from God. The patient answered, "Give me pain."

C. S. Lewis taught us that pain is God's megaphone, amplifying God's voice. In times of pain, we can hear God's voice more clearly than we would hear it otherwise.

There is recklessness in moving too fast, but pain can slow us down. Speed is important, but it can also be dangerous. The value of a good car doesn't depend on its speed, but on its safety, and safety depends on *controlled* speed. A thorn in the flesh can help us control the speed of our life.

A thorn in the flesh also helps us to keep the proper distance from others. We can learn the mystery of love from the hedgehog's dilemma. If hedgehogs get too close to each other to share heat in cold weather, they will hurt each other with their sharp quills. But if they remain too far apart, they will freeze in the bitter cold. They need each other, but they must maintain a certain distance to avoid pain. Likewise, our thorns help us maintain a proper distance from one another, drawing a boundary.

Spirituality is a matter of controlling the distance. Finding the balance between being alone and being with others is key. If we stay too close all the time, we get bored of each other. For intimacy we need a certain distance from time to time. When we move away from someone we care about, we miss that person. To love someone involves longing for that person.

Be thankful for the thorns in your life. But don't become a thorn to others. Being hurt by quills is better than hurting others.

Jesus was pierced by a crown of thorns and a spear on the cross. His blood healed many people who have suffered from thorns. It is curious how vaccines derived from harmful things can protect us from the damaging effects of those exact things. Likewise, it is Jesus' wounds that healed the wounds of many others, for he is the wounded healer.

Much like a rose that couples beauty with thorns, we know that this life has both wonder and pain. So let us be grateful for the thorn in the flesh and for the mysterious favor of God it allows. God uses the thorns for his good purposes, teaching us humility and dependence on him, transforming us into who he wants us to be.

# 9

# Vulnerability

*W*e need strength to persevere and prevail, so it seems natural for people to desire power in increasing increments. As we mature, we come to recognize the importance of power. Knowledge, health and money are equated with power. Competence, emotional intelligence, persuasive ability and influence are means to achieve those ends.

Even though power seems necessary, it is simultaneously dangerous. This is especially true of positional power, something very few are willing to relinquish. Oftentimes the more power used, the more desired. So this kind of power can easily be misused, leading us off track and straight toward destruction. When a person has too much power, multiple temptations must be confronted. The Roman philosopher Seneca said, "Man does not die. He kills himself." The abuse and overuse of power can be our downfall.

It is important for powerful people to limit the exercise of their power, intentionally becoming weaker. Spiritual training involves learning how to exercise self-control when it comes to the use of power. Failures and conflicts in relationships have a way of humbling us and curtailing our power. Sometimes we can be shaken and lose confidence when we feel weak, so weakness is another form of pain. However, if we use our weakness for good, it can be a blessing.

Through the turbulence and waves of the many difficulties in life, I became broken and weak. I have always fought weakness and vulnerability, but one day I realized that since I could not avoid the weakness, perhaps I could use it for growth. In that way, weakness can be an opportunity, a *blessing*, for in our weakness God reveals his strength.

Now, we should not *act* as if we are weak. Power in and of itself is neither good nor bad. But the problem arises when we lean on our own power first. When that happens, we don't leave room for God to intervene. Spiritual matters must be taken care of by spiritual power. If there's any human power involved in spiritual matters, there can't be any lasting spiritual fruit in it.

When we are weak and vulnerable, we rely on God. We put down our own strength and trust the Lord our God. In this way, we become united with God and develop intimate fellowship with him. Let us be thankful for our vulnerability, for vulnerability breeds humility, and humility helps us recognize our limits. And when we recognize our limits, we are able to become dependent on God.

In *Bread for the Journey*, Henri Nouwen says,

> There is a great difference between successfulness and fruitfulness. Success comes from strength, control, and respectability. A successful person has the energy to create something, to keep control over its development,

and to make it available in large quantities. Success brings many rewards and often fame. Fruits, however, come from weakness and vulnerability. And fruits are unique. A child is the fruit conceived in vulnerability, community is the fruit born through shared brokenness, and intimacy is the fruit that grows through touching one another's wounds. Let's remind one another that what brings us true joy is not successfulness but fruitfulness.

Jesus came as a tender shoot. A shoot is vulnerable, and its bud is soft. But the flowers and fruits come from that soft and tender bud, not the hard and strong branch. Yet abundant fruit only comes when those weak and vulnerable branches are united to the tree. In the same way, we bear fruit when we are united with Jesus. Spirituality involves maintaining that weak and vulnerable status so that we can trust God, not for success but for fruitfulness. Instead of whining and complaining about our weaknesses and vulnerabilities, let's be thankful for them.

# 10

# Deficiency

*W*hile there are many reasons to give thanks, we don't usually think of deficiency as one of them. But deficiency can be a vessel for God's grace. We long for a life of sufficiency, a life with no needs. But why is it that so many whose practical needs are met are so very often unhappy and unfulfilled? Perhaps it is because without deficiency there is no longing, and without longing there is no passion. So it is deficiency that gives birth to our desires, our longings, our dreams. Deficiency stirs our passion for God and for joy.

Abundance and achievement seem to be the ideal, but we know the pitfalls of emptiness and temptation that often follow success. Victory can make people arrogant, causing them to drop their guard. Thomas Carlyle once said, "Adversity is sometimes hard upon a man; but for one man who can stand prosperity, there are a hundred that will stand adversity."

The miracle at the wedding in Cana began with deficiency. Once the wine was gone the success of the celebration was threatened, so Mary came to Jesus and asked him for help. A deficiency paved the way for the miraculous. The same is true in our lives, which is why we can see deficiency as God's grace and as a reason for us to be thankful.

Once I saw a tall tree that had been planted long ago at a university by an American missionary. Because of its height it was the perfect target for lightning. The president of the university used the tree as an example of what can happen in our lives when *we* get too "tall" and as a reminder to lower ourselves in order to avoid being knocked down.

Jesus is God, but he humbled himself by becoming a human. He began with fullness, but he emptied himself and became a servant. He was strong in nature, but made himself vulnerable and weak, and became obedient even to the point of death. He *chose* to be deficient to be with us.

We can't survive on our own through self-sufficiency. Those who disagree have been deceived by their arrogance. We need one another and, more importantly, we need God. To think otherwise is a tragic mistake.

Imagine a candle lit in a bottle. To snuff out the light, all we have to do is to cover the bottle. Once the oxygen supply stops, the flame quietly dies. The same is true with our lives. If God stops supplying oxygen for us, even for a moment, we all die.

Like that candle, we all live in deficiency and dependence. But instead of resenting our deficiency, we can be thankful for it. My entire life has been lived "in need," and I believe God put me in that situation so I would rely on him and his providence alone. My deficiency has forced me to connect to God—but I know that my very survival is determined by this connection.

There is a Korean joke, "Those who walk cannot defeat those who run, those who run cannot defeat those who fly. But those who fly cannot defeat those who attach themselves to those who can fly." The wisest one among them is the one who attaches to the one who can fly. Being attached to God and to those who are blessed by God is true wisdom.

The world urges independence, but the Bible teaches us to be totally dependent on God. Let's not be ashamed of our dependence. Children are dependent on parents, and spouses are dependent on each other, so dependence is natural. Those who are dependent on God are the wisest ones.

Until they ran out of wine, no one knew or cared about who Jesus was. But in their deficiency, Jesus revealed himself to them. When we think we are sufficient, we might not feel God's presence, but when we are deficient we are able to better recognize God's presence in the midst of our lives. And there can be no greater happiness than encountering and experiencing God in our lives. So, then, our deficiency is a way of experiencing God's favor and should be a reason for gratitude. This is why I give thanks to God every day for my deficiency.

# 11

# Being Crumbled

*B*rokenness hurts, but being crumbled into many pieces is even more painful, since its force is greater than brokenness. The psalmist who experienced the pain of being crumbled said, "You have taken me up and thrown me aside" (Psalm 102:10).

At times we experience the pain of being crumbled or even crushed. Humans are like jars of clay, fragile and easily breakable, so we are susceptible to being crushed. But there is a special experience for those who reside in God's grace. God uses our brokenness and blesses us through our fracture. He renews us and re-creates us to become even more beautiful than before.

To realize that being crumbled may be an expression of God's grace is a blessing. Spiritual directors know that brokenness is God's way of bestowing his grace and shaping us into what he wants us to become. In *With Burning Hearts*, Henri Nouwen describes it this way:

I still remember an evening meditation on Dutch television during which the speaker poured water on hard, dried-out soil, saying, "Look, the soil cannot receive the water and no seed can grow." Then, after crumbling the soil with his hands and pouring water on it again, he said, "It is only the broken soil that can receive the water and make the seed grow and bear fruit."

After seeing this I understood what it meant to begin the Eucharist with a contrite heart, a heart broken open, to receive the water of God's grace.

To receive the water of God's grace, we must first allow God to break up the hard-dried soil of our hearts. Jesus taught us that the seed of the Word cannot take root in the rocky soil of a heart. In order for the seeds to take root, the rocky place must be tilled. And that tilling is often accomplished through suffering. Deep suffering breaks up the hard soil of the heart, allowing tears to flow. Such teardrops soften the soil of the human heart, allowing the seeds of God's Word to spring up and bear fruit in us.

The clay in a potter's hand comes from the breaking of hard soil. As the Great Potter, sometimes God re-creates us. Brokenness is essential for a new life to be born. During the birth process, water must break and blood comes out, breaking the womb in order to birth new life.

Pablo Picasso once said, "Every act of creation is first an act of destruction," but this "destruction" is intended for re-creation. In order for a caterpillar to soar as a butterfly, the caterpillar must experience brokenness. It must break through its chrysalis unassisted. If not, the butterfly will never develop the strength to fly. The butterfly must then leave behind the larva and abandon the chrysalis to fly away. It must empty itself of what was in order to become what God intends it to be. We can fly high through the process of brokenness, but in order to soar upward we may also need to leave something behind. No breaking, no emptying; no emptying, no re-creation.

Don't be tormented by brokenness. Instead, let's abandon our broken selves to God's masterful hands. By God's grace, brokenness can make us more beautiful and lighter so that we can fly. This is why we can endure pain and give thanks to God for being crumbled.

# 12

# Freedom to See the Good

*T*he power of gratitude is the ability to see the good. More specifically, a grateful person is *free* to see the good. When we give thanks, our eyes are opened and our hearts can understand. Simply having eyes doesn't guarantee sight. Eyes must be *opened* in order to see.

The reason we often don't see things correctly is that we see things as we *want* them to be, not as they really are. Most people are blinded by greed or desire, or their vision is skewed. But a grateful person is afforded a deeper understanding and the ability to see things as they are. Perspective is the ability to see with understanding, or have insight.

The same circumstance can stir up multiple viewpoints. The twelve spies sent to Canaan came back with conflicting reports. All went to the *same* land and saw the *same* people. The ten spies came back with very negative reports, intimidated by the land and the people of Canaan. But Joshua and Caleb described an exceedingly good land that flowed with milk and honey. All twelve saw the same land, yet they returned with two different sets of viewpoints: one with complaint and the other with gratitude. Joshua and Caleb were thankful for the land because they saw the good in it—because they saw it with God's perspective. We can be thankful to God when we see good things.

The ability to *see* good is the ability to *find* good. It is the power of gratitude that allows us to find good things where there seems to be none. Daniel knew that he would be thrown into the lions' den if he worshiped or prayed to the one true God, but he prayed and gave thanks as was the custom from his youth (Daniel 6:10). How could Daniel give thanks in that kind of circumstance? It was because he chose to focus on the greatness of his good God, his Protector whose powerful hand was with him in the midst of crisis.

Prayer and thanksgiving are holy partners. Giving thanks when we pray opens our spiritual eyes, allowing us to see further and deeper. Elisha's eyes were opened, so he was not panicked when the Syrian soldiers invaded; he saw the angel army surrounding him and protecting him (2 King 6:17).

Jesus prayed a prayer of thanksgiving in front of the tomb of Lazarus. The people saw a body that had been there long enough to stink, but Jesus saw God's glory. Jesus told Mary, "If you believe, you will see the glory of God" (John 11:40), after which he prayed a prayer of thanksgiving, for he saw the good things. Jesus saw the resurrection from that foul-smelling tomb, and he saw the glory of God.

God bestows the ability to see the unseen on those who have gratitude. The more thankful we are, the more good things there are to see. We can be thankful for all situations because we can *see* the good and *find* the good. This is why I begin each day by giving thanks.

# 13

# Slowness

*A*lthough speed is important, if one focuses too much on speed, danger awaits. The tragedy of the Titanic was created by the ship's reckless speed amid a field of icebergs. The captain's priority should have been the safety of the passengers, not the rate of travel; his ambition to arrive early resulted in the loss of many lives.

There are drawbacks to moving too slow, but usually less harm results from slowness. When we are too focused on speed we can easily lose our way. God isn't interested in how fast we move, but in our development toward maturity, so he often slows us down for our own good. Healthy growth takes time, so a life can only become beautiful through a slow process.

Many people despise slowness, but we can learn the wisdom of slowness. Being slow means to consider the process carefully. Being slow means to enjoy and taste the meaning of life. Being slow enables us to walk straight and not lose our direction. There is a kind of slowness that is persistent and not lazy, so a healthy person "hurries slowly."

Wise are those who are slow but persistent to continue good works. Completing the task is more important than doing it fast. There's nothing stronger than taking a step forward in meaningful work. Being fast is not strong. Being persistent is strong. Strong people walk consistently in the ways that God calls them to walk; it doesn't matter how fast or slow. We miss too many things when we move fast: we can't hear well, receive what we need, meet the people we should meet or experience the tender touch of God's hands. We must stop to hear his voice and find our rest in him.

Rushing around to try to carry out our own agendas can be very dangerous. God is not asking us to quickly carry out great tasks. He cares about the little things. Loving a soul quietly or caring for a wounded soul may seem insignificant, but these things are precious to God. American poet Emily Dickinson puts it this way in "Life":

If I can stop one heart from breaking,
I shall not live in vain;
If I can ease one life the aching,
Or cool one pain,
Or help one fainting robin into his nest again,
I shall not live in vain.

If God stops you when you move too fast, be thankful for this grace. We can experience a turning point in life when we slow down or stop. Even cars must slow down or stop to change directions. So when God slows us down or stops us, he is giving us an opportunity to check ourselves or turn around.

Stop and reflect now and then. Our souls get tired of moving too fast. Slow down and take care of your soul. Look into it quietly and feel the calmness. Then we can see the things we haven't seen before and understand things we never knew. This is why I am thankful for God's grace that slows me down.

Part Three

# The Power of Gratitude

# 14

# Learning to See the Little Things

When we are grateful, our eyes are opened to observe and be satisfied with even the littlest things, things that are easily taken for granted. We see infinite potential in them, helping us to see all things from the proper point of view.

A little thing can make an undetected difference that might then result in a huge difference. When we are grateful, we are like poets: we can see the things that others can't see. William Blake, an English poet, said it this way in "Auguries of Innocence":

> To see a World in a Grain of Sand
> And a Heaven in a Wild Flower,
> Hold Infinity in the palm of your hand
> And Eternity in an hour.

In order to see the small things, the wildflower or a grain of sand, we need to descend to the low places, to bow down. To see the universe and God's tears in a little dewdrop, to observe small things and tiny movements, one must stoop to look.

The Magi came to bow down before the baby Jesus and to worship him. They were willing to lower themselves in order to meet Jesus, and in that baby they recognized the hope of redemption for humanity. They saw the fullness of God.

Jesus used a tiny mustard seed to illustrate the kingdom of heaven, for there is an infinite future in a seed. In "History," Ralph Waldo Emerson said, "The creation of a thousand forests is in one acorn." Similarly, if one has kingdom eyes, a thousand trees can be seen in one seed.

Flowers are beautiful, but fruits are even more precious because seeds are in the fruits. Our lives are maintained and prolonged by things that come from tiny seeds. No matter how huge something may be, if there's no life in it, there is no future.

In order to experience the power of gratitude, we need to be interested in the little things, as Jesus was. He wanted the little ones to come to him. He praised the servant who was faithful with a little. And he was thankful for five small loaves and two small fish because he saw God's abundance in the little things.

God uses the humble person who values the little things. Mother Teresa, a small woman who saved many people with the love of Christ, described herself as a little pencil in the hand of a writing God. A small person *with* Jesus does a far greater work than a big person alone. God's interest is always in things that have been rejected, for there is nothing unimportant to God.

Let us be faithful with little things. Let us consider little ones precious and love them. Let us make this world beautiful by having gratitude for little things.

# 15

# Softening Hearts

*P*aul warns that the life of God cannot work in a hard heart (Ephesians 4:18), but gratitude has the power to soften hearts. When our hearts are hardened, we become insensitive (Ephesians 4:19) and unyielding (Exodus 9:7). A hardened heart will not listen. It might hear God's Word, but the Word makes no impression.

Our hearts often become hard because of wounds that have resulted in scars. As our hearts harden, they become narrow. A narrow mind does not have much capacity. On the other hand, as our hearts soften, they open up. Broad-minded people accept others well. Gratitude makes our hearts soft and open. That's why Paul asks us to "open wide your hearts" (2 Corinthians 6:13).

Joy is the fruit borne when something touches our heart, but a hardened heart cannot bear fruit. Kyung-Chul Jang, a theology professor at Seoul Women's University, says the antonym of joy is insensitivity. A hardened heart cannot feel any joy. Jesus compared this insensitive generation to children sitting in the marketplace: "We played the pipe for you, and you did not dance; we sang a dirge, and you did not mourn" (Matthew 11:17).

To be grateful is to be spiritually sensitive, and this has a softening effect on our hearts. Sensitive people show interest in little things. They are grateful for little things, impressed by little things. They cry over little things and rejoice in little things.

When something touches us, impression occurs. When there is impression, our heart moves, and that opens the door for joy. It springs up from within.

So gratitude begins with acknowledging what is given. In fact, much of what is necessary in our everyday lives is a free gift. We received our life for free. The very air we breathe is also free. There is nothing more precious than love. We can't buy love with money. It is a gift that suddenly came to us. It is grace and mystery. When we give thanks, we are able to open our eyes to the gifts we receive for free.

Thanksgiving can bring the moisture of tears to rain on the soil of our hearts. Tears of repentance and tears of thanksgiving are holy moisture that can soften even the hardest heart. When our hearts become soft, healing can begin.

When we give thanks, our hardened hearts become soft. We become sensitive and yielding. Our narrow minds get enlarged. And we experience joy as we give thanks. But, as we know from experience, giving thanks is not merely a result of our own efforts. It is a fruit of the Spirit. For that reason, we need to desire the Holy Spirit. We should make every effort to be open to God's grace. This is why I desire God's grace every day and seek his favor.

# 16

# Hope for the Hopeless

*G*ratitude is the ability to have hope in the midst of seeming hopelessness. Gratitude isn't a drug to escape or ignore the reality of desperate circumstances. Instead, it gives us the courage to confront our problems, offering hope where hope cannot be found.

The Bible teaches us to "give thanks in all circumstances" (1 Thessalonians 5:18). "All circumstances" means *all* circumstances, including the difficult times. This is incredibly difficult, yet when we give thanks in the midst of our trials and challenges, amazing things can happen.

Gratitude is a life skill and the application of God's wisdom. It is the means of holy living. There is an old saying, "Those who do battle without knowing the tactics will lose." In order to conquer the unwanted battles in our life, we should not neglect the strategies.

When we are in a situation where we see *nothing* to be thankful for, our perspective on the situation may change if we give thanks. Our attitudes can change, for in our gratitude we convey our trust of God and grow in wisdom.

Gratitude can keep us from being discouraged or over-whelmed by fear in the midst of a depressing situation. Even if the situation feels like a storm, for the sake of our family and neighbors, we need to discipline ourselves to keep calm.

Avoiding our frustrations and problems in the hopes of avoiding pain does not offer resolution. For that reason, we must confront our problems and do the hard work of pursuing solutions. Through the process, our faith grows, wisdom expands and character builds.

At times God allows problems in our lives and watches how we solve them, because God wants us to solve most of them on our own. God wants us to become people who can solve not only our own problems but also others.' But if we can't solve a problem after doing our best, then we must entrust it to God. Only then will God come to us to rescue us with his mighty hands.

We can find some inspiration from the prophet Habakkuk, who found hope in a hopeless situation. Habakkuk expressed gratitude in the midst of desperation, trembling as he waited for an invasion (Habakkuk 3:16). He was not ignorant of the reality, for it appeared as though there was nothing to rest his hope on. But he saw something that others couldn't see: God's saving hand, God's help. This is why he sang a song of hope: "Though the fig tree does not bud and there are no grapes on the vines, though the olive crop fails and the fields produce no food, though there are no sheep in the pen and no cattle in the stalls, yet I will rejoice in the LORD, I will be joyful in God my Savior" (Habakkuk 3:17-18).

We too can have courage in the midst of such circum-stances; we can be thankful because of our faith in God. Habakkuk confessed that "the righteous person will live by his faithfulness" (Habakkuk 2:4). God's people walk not according to circumstances but by faith in God. God has protected us thus far and is trustworthy to do so for the future.

Let us have hope during times that seem hopeless. Let us overcome the difficult times by faith in God.

# 17

# Tasting the Bitter and the Sweet

*G*ratitude gives us the ability to enjoy and the power to rejoice. Our maturity is revealed by what we enjoy. The psalmist delighted in the law of the Lord, meditating on it "day and night" (Psalm 1:2). David wrote, "Taste and see that the LORD is good" (Psalm 34:8). He delighted in God and wanted the people to do the same. Jesus delighted in the fear of the LORD (Isaiah 11:3), found joy in the Holy Spirit (Luke 10:21) and rejoiced over a lost soul being saved (Luke 15:7).

Spiritual discipline is needed for true pleasure. If we swallow without chewing, we cannot enjoy the taste of food. Similarly, we need to slow down in order to learn how to enjoy ourselves and others.

Gratitude is the ability to taste life. People have different personalities, intelligences and characteristics. In order to "taste" in our relationships, we must invest sufficient time. Only when we experience something deeply can we say we know its taste.

Hurry is the enemy of enjoyment. Deep taste requires much time. Expressing gratitude also takes time, because gratitude is the ability to express what we have "tasted" in words. Our expressions must be very specific, living and active, and that takes time.

Tasting deeply can move the heart. Expressions of love and gratitude come from the overflow of a heart that has been moved by and softened by gratitude.

Those who give thanks in all circumstances experience life as a gift, but that gift comes with both joy and sorrow wrapped in the same package, laughter and tears. The greatest joy cannot be tasted without tasting sufferings. Only those who have experienced anxiety know the importance of peace. Only those who have experienced depression know the blessing of delights.

Certain herbs have a bitter taste. It is interesting to note that the taste of bitter herbs intensifies the more we chew. We don't have to work hard to taste something sweet, but a bitter taste must be savored to be appreciated. The one who knows the taste of life knows the bitter taste of pain. But the deep taste of pain can't compare to the sweet taste of pleasure.

Many people sing out of their pain. Poets reflect this awareness. Their sufferings become the ingredients of their art. Song Mynghee is a famous poet in Korea who is handicapped by cerebral palsy. Her poems are filled with lofty songs that soar beyond her sufferings. Lee Jisun, whose body was 55 percent burned in an auto accident, writes and speaks to encourage others. There's always sweetness and the beauty of God in her writings. Those who can be grateful even for the difficult times are mature souls.

Sufferings and difficult times visit us like uninvited guests.

Instead of avoiding them, we need to face them and even embrace them. Give thanks to God for them. Then we shall know and taste the goodness of God.

# 18

# The Opportunity to Learn

*I* am grateful for the grace of learning. Jesus invited me to a place of learning when I accepted him as my personal Lord and Savior. "Take my yoke upon you and learn from me, for I am gentle and humble in heart, and you will find rest for your souls" (Matthew 11:29). An invitation to learn is an invitation to rest.

When I was young, learning was nothing but a painful labor, because I was not successful. But as I grew, I realized that learning is not limited to academic endeavors. After encountering Jesus, I got to know the meaning of true learning, which is not a source of pain but of joy. Learning renewed me and changed me for the better, growing me in maturity.

It is important that we learn how to learn. A Chinese proverb describes it this way: "Give a man a fish, and you feed him for a day; teach a man to fish, and you feed him for a lifetime." Great teachers help their students learn how to learn. In *What Is Called Thinking*, Martin Heidegger reminds us what is required of great teachers:

The teacher is ahead of his apprentices in this alone, that he has still far more to learn than they—he has to learn to let them learn. The teacher must be capable of being more teachable than the apprentices. The teacher is far less assured of his ground than those who learn are of theirs.

I learned how to learn as I read, but we don't read only books. We can read God, life, people's hearts and even nature. We can even read ourselves. As I read the Bible, I learned that the Bible is also "reading" me. Through learning, we discover our true selves and become more mature versions of ourselves. This discovery, to now know something we didn't know before and to put that into words, is a precious experience. It can cause our souls to dance.

To discover understanding or enlightenment requires openness. As soon as one's mind develops an opening, understanding flows into it. If that understanding flows through to others, it becomes delightful. Learning enables communication with others and enhances the abundant life, which leads to contentment.

Learning is such a precious experience for me because every experience and incident can be an opportunity for discovery and understanding. Sufferings make life hard, but they can be very good teachers. Of course, I don't enjoy sufferings, but I have to admit that I learn much more from suffering than I do from times of comfort and ease. And sometimes my sufferings return to teach different lessons for different seasons of my life.

I have tasted the bitter of life during the hard times. But it was a deep, life-changing taste. Those deep tastes have never been wasted. God placed joy, sadness, success, failure, victory and defeat together in one gift package called "life."

I feel that I am aging these days, so I am trying to develop the most difficult art and skill of aging well. Henri-Frédéric Amiel, a Swiss writer known for his masterpiece *Journal in Time*, once said this: "To know how to grow old is the masterwork of wisdom, and one of the most difficult chapters in the great art of living." It is important to learn how to grow old well because it will make not only our lives abundant but also the lives of those around us.

Let us open ourselves to learning, that we might be thankful for God's grace of learning and continue to learn how to learn all of our days.

# 19

# The Gift of Time

*T*ime is God's gift. I used to think that people who say, "Time heals all wounds" were making an excuse to avoid their problems. But as I grow older I have discovered that I agree with this statement and find it to be a very meaningful maxim left to us by our ancestors.

Humans are weak, vulnerable and easily wounded. The pain of loss, abandonment, betrayal and failure can drive us into a whirlpool of frustration. But slowly and gradually, as time goes by, we gain energy to stand firm. Time heals the wounds, and peace settles in the hearts of those whose hope is deeply rooted.

Time is a gift because it helps us grow. All the problems we considered serious when we were young lose significance as we age. How does this happen? The problems don't change at all, but our perspectives do. As we grow older we gain wisdom and skills to face our problems and resolve our conflicts. Time offers us the gift of experience revealed in maturity.

As we mature we start to acknowledge our limits. Young

people often behave unwisely, thinking problems can be over-powered. But we learn that the exertion of too much strength can cause problems. We also learn that what appears to be weakness is often strength in disguise and that softness is often better than might.

Only when we are able to accept the fact that we are aging can we get on the road to maturity. To be mature means to know the seasons of life, and to know the seasons of life is to know the ways of life. When we understand those ways, wisdom begins to permeate our lives.

As time goes by, we learn that life is filled with paradox. Some things we thought were wrong turn out to be beneficial. Prayers we thought were rejected by God turned out to be his blessings. We find that God pours his grace on us and turns our mistakes into his blessings.

Sometimes those to whom we are closest can wound us the deepest, while strangers surprise us with blessing. But we grow in maturity and humility, growing more like Christ through our failures, challenges and hurts.

One of the most precious gifts that time gives us is the gift of knowing Jesus more deeply. We are blessed by the precious gift of God's son, and to know him deeper over time is a great joy.

Since we can't stop the passing of time, let us learn to enjoy it. Time went by even today, and the gifts that time gave me are in my hands now, so I am thankful for God's gifts today.

# 20

## The Shadow of God's Hand

We can be thankful for a shadow. There are times when it seems like a dark shadow covers our life in sadness. In these times, the full force of light is blocked, and we are left experiencing a certain kind of darkness, much like a tunnel. There might be plenty of light outside, and we may even be intellectually aware of that light, but we are not experiencing the light. We feel stuck in the darkness, imprisoned or isolated by the shadow. And nothing seems to be working. Inevitably, our hearts rush and hurry, but all we can do is wait.

In hindsight, we sometimes see that those shadowed days were in fact blessed days. We realize that we grew more mature and put down deeper roots because of those dark days. And we recognize the shadow to be the shadow of God's hand.

In order to protect us, God sometimes puts us under the shadow of his hand. The prophet Isaiah put it in this way:

> He made my mouth like a sharpened sword,
> in the shadow of his hand he hid me;

he made me into a polished arrow
  and concealed me in his quiver. (Isaiah 49:2)

When I was young, there was no electricity in my village, so we used a gas lamp at home. I remember that I would often protect the lid with one hand to keep the flame alive. Perhaps you have done the same thing while walking with a candle. As the Bible says, "A smoldering wick he will not snuff out" (Isaiah 42:3). We are like smoldering wicks. Sometimes we seem so vulnerable and weak that even a tiny wind can put out the light. That's when God carefully puts his hand over us to cover us, protecting us until our fire is strong again.

God knows that we need both sunshine and shadow in our lives. In *Highways of the Heart*, George Morrison says, "It is one of the great offices of faith to take the shadowed seasons of the life and to reckon them the shadow of His hand." When we need his shadow, God never removes it from us too soon. He continues to protect and strengthen us in the midst of the shadow until our flame is once again burning strong.

God's people are protected and prepared for the future under the shadow of God's hand. When Joseph ran away from the temptation of Potiphar's wife, he was put into prison. During these years, the shadow of God's hand protected Joseph, growing him in maturity and preparing him for his assigned role.

God often puts us under the shadow so we can experience the truly abundant life. There are times when God stops our progress so that he can entrust us with more important tasks. Sometimes he pulls us back from where we used to be.

Those who grow in maturity while under a shadow are uniquely qualified to encourage other people in a similar situation. Spiritual giants all grow up under the shadow. For that reason, those giants know how to minister to people who need rest. How great it is to know that the shadow in our life is in fact the shadow of God's hand!

I dare to encourage those who are struggling through a time in the shadows. Don't be discouraged! Prepare for a bright future under the shadow of God's hand. And remember, when you come out of the shadow, the light on your face will be brighter than ever!

# 21

# The Grace to Restart

*A* wonderful aspect of grace is that it allows us to start all over. The last few years were rough for me. At times I felt as if I were in a dark tunnel, filled with fear that I would never see light again. Despair means to lose hope. Discourage means to lose courage. Both put us in a place psychologically where it seems like we can never start again.

When does our hope arise? Our God is the God of hope, and he offers us the message that we can start all over. That's the essence of the gospel. What good news! The grace that God showed us on the cross is the grace that allows us to start over. The cross has the power to help us not only leave the past behind but transcend it and march forward into the future.

Even at the edge of a cliff, God helps us to restart. In fact, God does some of his best work on the precipices of life. The resurrection began at the edge of the cross, so we learn that the end is not really the end. In the poem *Little Gidding*, T. S. Elliot says,

What we call the beginning is often the end.
And to make an end is to make a beginning.
The end is where we start from.

God often provides us with a new encounter after the sorrow of a difficult farewell. He opens a new door as we experience the pain of failure. But in order to restart, we must be good at closing the door on the past. Closing the door means acknowledging our failures and losses. Closing the door might also mean recognizing and repenting of sin, or forgiving those who have hurt us. Only then will new encounters begin.

At the end of every year, we celebrate New Year's Eve. We say goodbye even as we say hello to another year. It is God's grace that we can welcome a new year. Every turn of the calendar page (years, months, weeks, days) provides us with a new beginning.

When we start over, we need to restore our hearts afresh. Farmers begin a new season by sowing seeds. Farmers till the fields, sow seeds and plant new plants every year as if they were doing it all for the first time. In a sense, that is exactly what they are doing. Each sowing produces new plants in their season.

When God gives us a new year, a new month or a new day, it means that God wants us to end the past properly and start over. The most beautiful day is the day to come. Let us welcome a new day with excitement for a new start.

# 22

# The Importance of Roots

*G*od's wisdom is often revealed in the pattern and flow of nature. Roots are the most significant part of the tree, but they are invisible. Hidden. Yet they determine the future of a tree. Roots have three functions: anchoring, storage and supply. When the roots are deep, trees can endure under nearly any circumstance. Likewise, the level of storage determines the size of the future supply. If there's no storage, there will be no supply.

In a cold winter season, although trees are not externally active, they are very busy internally. This is the wisdom of trees, for during the winter months they take care of their roots, growing them and storing up their energy. As winter becomes spring, that energy stored in the roots spurs on the external activity of sprouts and branches, flowers, buds and fruit. In other words, there is spring in the roots of the winter tree.

The depth of the roots determines the strength of the tree. Height can be deceiving, for if a tree has shallow roots it can be easily toppled by a storm. But deep-rooted trees will not be shaken. So when do trees send their roots deeply into the soil? It is during times of famine. When there are abundant waters, trees can survive with shallow root growth. But during times of drought or after a big fire on the mountain area, trees can only absorb fresh water by sending their roots deeply into the ground.

In order to strengthen our roots, God allows suffering in our lives. He allows drought, fire and winter in our lives so that we can deepen our roots in him. It is during our times of thirst and threat that we strive after living water. In these times we tend to pay attention to the inner world of our souls. Oftentimes when there is much external activity we neglect our internal world. For that reason, sometimes God allows a very cold winter in our life when we need to tend our souls.

When the cold winter comes to our life, all the external activity stops. The visitors stop coming, and the invitations stop rolling in. Popularity is gone. That leaves us only one thing to do: take care of the roots of our inner world and start to become a mature person. We shouldn't waste our winter, because it won't last forever. This is the time that we should send our roots deeply to God, who is the source of living water (Jeremiah 17:8). This way we are able to store up divine strength even as we look forward to spring's return.

Roots are sometimes like barns, for they also store, save and accumulate. We think of Joseph, who stored up the harvest so there was sufficient supply during the seven years of famine. But barns are not only for storage. They also can be clearinghouses for sharing. Those with full barns are enabled to trade with others, to meet various needs. Abundant storage leads to abundant sharing. A winter season is sad and painful for those who are poor and lonely. Despite our own winter season of life, we can experience a season of grace that takes care of our roots and allows us to store up blessings for future use.

We can be thankful in the winter season, as it is meant to be a season of God's favor to tend to our roots, and look forward to an abundant spring.

# 23

# Shaping Our Relationships

*L*ife is a series of encounters with other people who shape our lives. Consciously and unconsciously, we are influenced by the perspectives, values, virtues, attitudes, languages and even the dress of those with whom we fellowship. In this sense, our encounters determine the quality of our lives.

But Paul's admonishment still applies to us today: "Do not be misled: 'Bad company corrupts good character'" (1 Corinthians 15:33). Since our encounters with others will always result in change, and our lives are the product of our previous encounters, we must be discerning. It is illogical to expect a good result from a bad choice, yet we are so often surprised by the consequences resulting from our liaisons.

But God's purposes for relationship are revealed in the wisdom of his Word:

As iron sharpens iron,
    so one person sharpens another. (Proverbs 27:17)

God provides us with the opportunity for encounter and relationship with good teachers, good students, good friends and good spouses. But the choice is ours. And the fellowship that we choose is like a seed that will eventually bear fruit.

Through Jesus' example, we can learn how to make good choices for our relationships. Before Jesus chose the twelve disciples from among many people, he *prayed* (Luke 6:12-13).

Genuine fellowship is God's gracious gift to us. However, it is still our responsibility to cultivate and maintain these relationships. This care will make a lasting impact. More than anything else, the secret to maintaining these relationships is gratitude, for such a spirit is attractive to others. It has the subtle power to make people stay long.

Even though these encounters with others transform us, there is an even more significant encounter, a mysterious encounter. Until I had a mysterious encounter with Jesus, I didn't know the potential within me. Although I was still young, I was aware of my sin and cried and cried to repent. That encounter—that *relationship*—has changed my entire life. I was chosen by God, and I decided to trust in his grace with my whole heart. Making the choice to trust means that we choose our future. The day I chose to trust God was a blessed day that affected the course of eternity.

Part Four

## The Spiritual Gifts
of Gratitude

# 24

# The Wisdom of Letting Go

*I*n our lives we frequently face the decision of whether to hold on or let go. There often seems to be wisdom in holding on. When we grasp opportunities, connections with influential people, money, real estate, honor or power, we consider it a blessing. However, it is ironic that oftentimes we do not grasp these things but are grasped by them. The very things we think will bring joy can bring misery, and the things we think will bring freedom only enslave us.

There is a story told in Africa and India about a technique the natives use to catch monkeys. They hollow out one end of a coconut and put in some peanuts. The monkey puts its hand in the coconut, and when it makes a fist to grab the peanuts, it is trapped. The natives then pull a string attached to the other end of the coconut, and the monkey is captured. In truth, the monkey was never trapped, since all it had to do was let go of the peanuts, but sometimes letting go is much more difficult than grasping.

To live by faith means to live a life of constant letting go.

Growth, maturity and renewal *require* us to let go of the old.

When God initially encountered Abram, he required Abram to let go of all the things that he had depended on. Abram had to let go of his old land in order to get to the land God had promised to him. In order to become the father of faith, he had to let go of his old, pagan way of life.

God promised Abram a son and a great nation from his descendants. As a sign of the promise, God changed Abram's name to Abraham ("father of a multitude"). But that promise was not realized right away, so Abraham had his own idea of how this promise should be fulfilled. First he clung to his nephew, Lot. After Lot left, Abraham clung to his servant Eliezer. Later he clung to Ishmael, whom he had through Hagar. But God wanted Abraham to let go even of Ishmael. Finally Abraham had Isaac, and the true promise of God was realized.

After Abraham released everything he had previously relied on and instead grasped Isaac, God commanded him to let go of Isaac too. That was a painful test for Abraham, but he passed. When he decided to offer Isaac as an offering at Mount Moriah, he finally opened both of his hands and released his grasp on the way he thought things should be. He let go of Isaac. That's when the ram appeared. It was in the experience of letting go that Abraham finally became a free man. God returned Isaac to Abraham's empty hands, but Abraham didn't cling to Isaac any longer. That day Abraham became united with God and became God's friend; that day he began to cling to God.

Letting go is not just a matter of giving something up. Instead letting go is a desire to be one with God. Those who hold tightly to everything, even to the end of life, become miserable people. At the moment of dying, we relinquish everything. But we need to practice letting go before that day comes.

We can practice letting go of our wealth, health, relationships, sexuality, power and even our egocentric self. When we let go of the things we are attached to, we can enjoy true rest in God's bosom. When we let go of external matters, such as material prosperity, we can go deeper into internal matters and the richness that God has prepared for us. Letting go is wisdom and grace.

Let go of the past, which you cannot change. Stop clinging to anything that is not God. This is how you can reach freedom and find your true self. We must practice letting go while we are still young so we can be more free to share when we grow older.

I am practicing letting go every day. But I have to confess that in my frail humanity, it is always a struggle to let go. May God help us all to let go.

# 25

# Solitude

*I* don't enjoy solitude, but I am thankful for it. Solitude can sometimes be the source of tremendous pain. It is perhaps the primary reason many of us fear growing old: we don't want to be left alone in the end. But solitude cannot be avoided, and there is much to be learned from it, so we might as well become familiar with it lest we suffer from a sudden and unexpected encounter with it one day. Being familiar with solitude means that one becomes familiar with one's self. Blessed are those who feel comfortable with themselves.

When I began meditation for soul care, the time alone was very difficult. Facing myself honestly in the solitude was terribly awkward and uncomfortable. I was caught up in my false self, and though I realized I didn't like it very much, I didn't want to encounter my true self. Courage was required to face myself in those times of solitude.

We should not avoid solitude but learn to embrace it, for it can give us depth of insight and wisdom in return. It helps us to delve into our inner world, avoiding shallowness and growing in maturity.

During moments of solitude, our souls become poor. Solitude takes us to silence, and when we become silent, we find that world to be deep. Of course, many problems occur when silence is broken. Immature language and emotions that don't endure the silence can cause many problems. But enduring silence helps us care for the inner flame. It helps our language ripen. It also takes us to God, helping us develop a heart for him.

We desire God in the solitude, for it leads us to the deeper inner sanctuary where we encounter him. Silence ushers us into the world of God's mystery. It is solitude that helps us to go deeper into a place of inner rest. It is in solitude that we can fully experience God's embrace.

Regardless of our possessions or achievements, solitude takes us to a position where we can be enough simply by existence. Erich Fromm's book *To Have or To Be?* divides life into two categories: "to have" and "to be." What makes us abundant and generous is "to be," so we must train ourselves to be content with "to be." That contentment comes when we become familiar with solitude.

Children who know how to play alone learn not to fear being alone as adults. Adults who do not fear being alone know how to give others their own space and time, to not exert pressure in circumstances or relationships. They are able to love others not only with what they *have* but with who they *are*, because love is not about having but about being.

When you are in solitude, don't be too lonely. When you feel lonely, go deeper into the encounter with God. The God we meet in the still, quiet place will calm us and comfort us.

It is not about external riches; it is all about internal richness. God should be the eternal home of our heart. This is why I am thankful to the God who gave me solitude as a gift.

# 26

# Encouragement

*I* suffered despair while going through hardship. Despair is often followed by discouragement, which can easily lead to burnout. Burnout is like running out of fuel for the inner flame. When the lantern is out of fuel it burns only the wick, which produces smoke but no light. When we "burn the wick" in our lives, we can suffer extreme disappointment and fatigue. It is during these times that we often face serious temptation. We can become depressed and want to give up. Life feels like it has no meaning, putting us in grave danger.

In *How to Influence People*, John Maxwell and Jim Dornan remind us that "few things help a person the way encouragement does." In fact, "George M. Adams called it 'oxygen to the soul.'" When you light a candle and place it in a glass bottle, oxygen keeps the flame burning. If you cover the bottle with a lid, the oxygen supply is cut off, and the fire will die out.

There is a flame in our inner world too. Encouragement is the oxygen that keeps this flame burning brightly. When life gets difficult and we are starving for encouragement, we begin to fade and burn out. When we are encouraged, we gain strength and can move again.

The word "encouragement" has its root in "courage." To encourage is to put courage into someone. To put energy into a person. Most people live without conviction, and so many are discouraged. Sometimes even those who seem successful suffer from feelings of inferiority. So everyone needs encouragement to restore energy.

I know what it is to wallow in the swamp of depression. I am so thankful for the encouragement I received during that time; it was the hand of God that pulled me out.

I have never seen a person who doesn't need encouragement. Every person—every day—needs support from others. It is as basic to our survival as our need for food, water and oxygen. The more abundant the supply of loving support, the more we thrive. And in our abundance, we can then share with others in need.

The right kind of encouragement helps us to try something new. It can also enable us to persevere—to take just one more step. When we are doing something good and important, there aren't always immediate results. Parents and teachers face such a challenging and tiring task. But encouragement holds the power to help them press on.

Encouragement can also help us restart certain endeavors we may have given up on. Sometimes it takes much more energy to restart something than it does to maintain something, so we need encouragement to finish well without faltering. Many noble tasks have been left incomplete due to a lack of encouragement. As we all know from experience, life is not a sprint; it is a marathon, which is why we should not hurry or rush too much.

Encouragement can mean cheering someone up. We know the power of a letter or a card with warm words and a small gift. "And let us consider how we may spur one another on toward love and good deeds" (Hebrews 10:24). Let us keep those encouraging words that we received during our hard times and share them with our neighbors who are going through their own hard times.

Ultimately, we are thankful for the Holy Spirit, who is our Encourager and our Anointer. Through Scripture, encounters with good people and encouragement to fix our eyes on Jesus, the Holy Spirit restores and strengthens us. And then, when we live the life of an encourager, we become imitators of God. This is why the life of an encourager is beautiful.

# 27

# Rebuilding Broken Bridges

*G*ratitude has the ability to connect people to God and to one another. In fact, it has the power to build new bridges and to repair broken relationships, even those that seem irreparably damaged.

Sin breaks all things, creating separation from God and others. It is born out of our desire and greed, eventually bringing forth death (James 1:15). The biblical definition of death is separation. Because of the sin of Adam, humans are separated from God. Because of our disconnection, we fall into despair, condemnation and judgment. Sin doesn't just break the bridge; it burns it.

Jesus came to the earth to repair humanity's broken relationship with God. The cross is the point of connection, the place where broken bridges are rebuilt and restored. Through the cross we receive the abundant life that can only come through a right relationship with God (John 10:10).

In the Old Testament, God anointed priests to bridge the gap between people and himself. In *Worship His Majesty*, Jack Hayford explains it well:

*Pontifex* is the Latin word for priest. The beauty of the word is that by its actual derivation it makes clear that priest is an active idea, its history revealed in a word of positive and powerful purpose. The real meaning lies in the original definition of "pontifex": "bridge builder." The etymology of the word undergirds such English words as "pons" (a bridge), "pontage" (the toll for crossing the bridge) and "pontoon" (a floating bridge). . . . Priesthood was always meant to be something practical—to help us cross over, or to get from here to there.

Priests interceded for the people so they could connect to God. They built bridges between God and people through sin and thanksgiving offerings. The Old Testament priests are a pretype of Jesus. Jesus is *the* Priest in the order of Melchizedek; Jesus is the bridge-builder.

We know what destroys and disconnects our relationships: things like anger, resentment, criticism, hostility, a vengeful heart or refusing to forgive. These are dangerous bridge burners because once a bridge is burned, there is no going back. Because of our human nature, we will have conflict. But we should never lose hope for reconciliation and forgiveness, so we should always try to leave ourselves room to return.

Gratitude holds the power of restoration because it begins with the forgiveness we receive from God. That forgiveness is found in the love shown at the cross.

Through deep-rooted thanksgiving, we can forgive others. When we give thanks, our hearts and eyes are opened to see the good in other people. We begin to see infinite potential in them, and we come to respect them. When our relationships with others are reconnected through gratitude, the flow of life becomes abundant.

The essence of God's life is love. For that reason, the more abundant life, the more abundant love. We are a royal priesthood, so our mission is to establish a bridge. Those bridges are established through thanksgiving. We can make this world a place where God's eternal life is overflowing through gratitude.

# 28

# The Power of Expression

*G*ratitude is an expression of appreciation, an articulation of what we have received. Like a receipt, our gratitude is evidence of the transaction of grace from God.

The beautiful sound of a bell is not known until it rings. In the same way, the beauty of an instrument is not known until it is played. And love is not love unless it is expressed. We who have experienced love know just how marvelous it is. Love is a thick, deep feeling. It is echo, vibration and wavelength. Sometimes it involves heartache and pain. But a love relationship only begins when love is expressed.

People who neglect the importance of expression or articulation do not yet know real life. It is the power of language that moves people, and how something is expressed determines whether it results in communication or conflict. How to speak, what to speak, when to speak and to whom we speak can change our lives. Language has the power of creation, touching and moving people's hearts.

Prayer also involves language. When we pray, God listens

and responds. And our faith is revealed through our confession. When Jesus heard the confession of the centurion, he praised his faith. Words have power.

God works according to our expression. When our thoughts are expressed in words, they become powerful energy. No matter how hard this world is, when we use language well, it can be a more beautiful place. We all can be happy. Of course, humanity does not live by language alone; we also need bread to eat. But we cannot overemphasize the power of words.

We know well the story of the ten lepers in Luke 17. Jesus healed ten lepers, but only one came back to thank Jesus. In fact, he—a Samaritan—threw himself at Jesus' feet and praised God in a loud voice.

Of course, the nine others were thankful to be healed, but they didn't return to express their gratitude. And gratitude only has power when it is expressed.

Because gratitude flows out of deep thought and understanding, it raises one's power of expression. For this reason, the language of gratitude can move the hearts of many people.

When gratitude is expressed, our hearts are opened. When our hearts are opened, we want to share more love and grace with others. In the same way, God bestows more love and grace on us when we thank him.

Those who can express gratitude under difficult circumstances reveal maturity. That kind of gratitude is like Habakkuk's attitude of appreciation, or that of Paul while in prison.

Let us express gratitude. There isn't a financial expense, so it's something we can all afford to do. Let us choose gratitude over blame, for gratitude is like a magnet that attracts the better things. Expressions of gratitude deepen our love for and relationship with God and others.

# 29

# Creative Responsiveness

*K*arl Menninger once said, "Attitudes are more important than facts." What he meant is that we become sad or unhappy *not* because of what actually happened but because of our attitudes. We can't control what happens to us, but we can control our attitudes and responses.

With a proper attitude, anything experienced can become a blessing. But how can we respond appropriately? We need to allow God's perspective to filter our interpretation of any given situation. We need his sovereign and eternal perspective on everything.

Joseph is a great example of this, because he didn't resent his brothers, who sold him into slavery. In fact, he forgave and blessed them instead. This was only possible because Joseph interpreted and responded to his circumstances with God's perspective.

Gratitude gives us this ability to respond creatively, for it offers us God's perspective. Without God's perspective, we can't give thanks in all things. Believing God's sovereign plans are reflected in all circumstances and choosing to respond positively is the attitude of gratitude. With that kind of attitude, we have the power to respond creatively, no matter what happens.

In *The Courage to Create*, Rollo May says, "Human freedom involves our capacity to pause between the stimulus and response and, in that pause, to choose the one response toward which we wish to throw our weight." Even though the situation at hand stimulates a response, we can pause before acting. That pause creates a space for choice. Korean writer Shinyoung Cho calls that space a "cushion."

An immature person reacts to an incident when there is *any* stimulus. That person might act emotionally and impulsively, being easily annoyed by and blaming others. On the other hand, a mature person can pause to think and interpret the situation from God's perspective, then have the ability to respond creatively, with gratitude.

We all have this ability to pause between stimulus and response and to make a wise choice, but what is required in that moment of pause is responsibility. We are not responsible for everything that happens to us, but we are responsible for choosing how to interpret and respond as a mature individual.

There are many unwanted things that we can't keep from happening to us along life's journey. When we respond with a biblical perspective and are able to give thanks in all things, our spiritual eyes are opened. This is a creative response that allows us to discover the treasures that are often hidden in darkness. When we give thanks, that light shines, allowing us to see new and great things.

Gratitude enables us to see the paradoxical blessings hidden in even the most difficult of circumstances. This helps us to endure better and respond to problems creatively. We can experience the mysterious growth that can be found only in going through hardship.

Let us choose gratitude during the pause between stimulus and response. And let us respond to difficult situations creatively, with gratitude. Then we can experience God's hand, which changes our sadness into joy.

# 30

# Obstacles

Obstacles are any form of a barrier that blocks our way. Weakness, incidents, timing, suffering or people can all bring us to a stop. But when we see these obstacles from God's perspective, then we can recognize them as reasons for gratitude.

Obstacles have a way of stopping us in our tracks. Knowing how to stop is an important life skill. A person who doesn't know how to stop is like a car without a brake system; both are a danger to everyone around. Sometimes God allows us to face obstacles when we need to stop. It is his blessing to stop us before things get worse. But these obstacles are not meant to make us give up. They are to help us control our speed and check our direction. And sometimes we find we need to lay down our own agendas to recalibrate our direction and purpose.

Obstacles also reveal our level of determination. If an obstacle keeps us from pursuing something we want, that means we didn't want it very badly. In his book *The Last Lecture*

Randy Pausch says, "Brick walls are there for a reason. They give us a chance to show how badly we want something." The brick walls aren't there to keep us out but can reveal our deepest desires.

Obstacles can be instruments of God's blessing to bring us clarity. Henry Ford said, "Obstacles are those frightful things you see when you take your eyes off your goal." We can easily lose sight of our goals, but sometimes the obstacles help us refocus.

As we face obstacles, we discover that the challenge is not in the obstacles themselves but in our lack of dependence on God. We come to realize that the only way to overcome obstacles is to walk with God, who is greater than any problem. And as we practice this dependence, we grow in wisdom and maturity.

In 1952 Sir Edmund Hillary failed in his attempt to climb Mount Everest. In response he called out to the great mountain, "I will defeat you yet. . . . Because you are as big as you are going to get—but I'm still growing." Not long after, he became the first man to successfully reach the summit. Sometimes obstacles encourage us to keep growing.

Jack Parr, an American talk show host, once said, "Looking back, my life seems like one long obstacle race, with me as the chief obstacle." We often think that obstacles are the problem, but we ourselves are the main problem. Our perspective regarding obstacles is more important than the obstacles themselves. If we see obstacles from God's point of view and treat them with gratitude, obstacles are tools of God's favor.

Nick Vujicic was born with tetra-amelia syndrome, a rare disorder characterized by the absence of all four limbs. But his handicap has not blocked his future. In fact, he is using his handicap as a tool for motivating people and sharing the gospel as an evangelist. As a result of his "obstacle," he shares hope with many other people.

No matter how difficult the obstacle, we should not let it defeat us. God does not allow obstacles in order to discourage us but to grow us. They are given so that we can have victory with our God, who is bigger than any obstacle in our lives. This is why we should be thankful even for the obstacles.

# 31

# Transforming the Mundane

*I*n their book *Sparks of Genius*, Robert and Michèle Root-Bernstein say, "The greatest insights often come to individuals who are able to appreciate the 'sublimity of the mundane,' the deeply surprising and meaningful beauty in everyday things." In order to discover the dignity of everyday life in ordinary days, it helps to have an attitude of gratitude.

People who give thanks all the time have great insight and great observational power. This allows them to give thanks for the small and ordinary things others don't see. They recognize the value and the miraculous in the ordinary, often through tears.

Jesus took the five little loaves and two insignificant fish and prayed a prayer of thanksgiving. Gratitude attracts miracles, and those small things—offered to God with gratitude—became sufficient food to feed thousands.

Jesus saw the miraculous in the mundane because he viewed everything with an eternal perspective. He saw the kingdom of heaven in a mustard seed (Matthew 13:31). He taught that one soul has greater value than the whole world (Matthew 16:26) and that whatever is done to "the least of these" is done to him (Matthew 25:40). Jesus saw something magnificent in Peter, who trembled like a reed but would become solid as a rock.

Once we open our eyes to the sublimity of the mundane, everything seems to be miraculous. Albert Einstein said, "There are only two ways to live your life. One is as though nothing is a miracle. The other is as though everything is a miracle." People of gratitude consider everything to be miraculous.

As G. K. Chesterton famously wrote, "We are perishing for lack of wonder, not for lack of wonders." One grain of rice will produce 180 rice grains. When planted, one potato produces about sixty potatoes. One female salmon contains more than three thousand eggs. There are thousands of oak trees in one acorn. To sow a tiny black watermelon seed and see a harvest of hundreds of watermelons is to witness the miraculous. Every day we are surrounded by God's abundance and his magnificence; miracles aren't things we *create* but what we *discover* and *experience*.

To whom are miracles happening? Miracles happen to those who are faithful during ordinary times and place value in the little things. It was a miracle that defeated Goliath with a small stone. But we must remember that the miracle was not performed *by* David, but happened *to* him.

Miracles are not far from us. They are near us in our everyday lives. Let us be thankful for our ordinary days and little things. Let us remember that miracles can happen when we value little talents and exercise them faithfully. With gratitude, let us live out the sublimity of the mundane.

# 32

# Humility

## *The Root of Gratitude*

*H*umility is the root of gratitude. Unlike flowers that can grow in shallow ground, gratitude takes root in the deep, beautiful soil of humility. The humble even give thanks for and find meaning in small things. Nothing is taken for granted, because life itself is a wonder.

When we view the world through humble eyes, it is full of wonder. Even the road we walk is a wonder. But because our eyes are looking for the big things, we often miss the ordinary miracles found on the street before us. The power of gratitude helps us discover things we can be thankful for in our everyday lives.

Being grateful is to be struck with admiration by the little things. In Chinese, there is an expression for extreme gratitude called "marvelous admiration." It is considered gratitude for excellence. It seems logical to admire the excellent, but who can admire the small or seemingly insignificant? Only the humble.

Mahatma Gandhi said, "One must become as humble as the dust before he can discover truth." When we recognize God's immensity and consider ourselves in comparison, we are humbled by how small we really are.

When we are humbled to a low place, we discover hidden wonders. Look at the wildflowers in a field. Grasp the hands of little children. When we humble ourselves, anything around us can look big and wonderful. But when we think more of ourselves than we should and consider all else insignificant, we're not grateful for anything.

Abraham referred to himself as nothing but dust when he prayed (Genesis 18:27). What a humble expression! Abraham could refer to himself as nothing but dust since God told him that God would make his offspring as numerous as the dust of the earth (Genesis 13:16). Abraham embraced God's language as his own and humbly embraced God's promise. Abraham realized that a person who is like dust can be the basis of great family if God wills.

Gratitude is an expression of appreciation for the things that are given to us. Essentially, it is the discovery of the existing things—things we already have—and giving meaning and value to them. In *The Life and Strange Surprising Adventures of Robinson Crusoe of York*, Daniel Defoe said that the reason we are not satisfied in spite of our lack is that we are not thankful for the things we have. Humble people know what they already have and give thanks.

There is a Chinese proverb that says that we should remember the source of the water when we drink it. If we remember the source of our water, then we can be thankful. If we remember the work and sweat of the farmers who provide the food we eat, then we can be thankful. And if we remember

God, who provides the seeds, sunshine and rain accordingly to farmers so we can eat our meals, we can be thankful.

We are not the source of the good things we have. God is our only source. In fact, God is the spring of living water (Jeremiah 17:13). This is why we can give thanks to the Lord every day.

Part Five

# The Path to Gratitude

# 33

# The Key of Prayer

*A*s God's people, prayer is his grace and our privilege. At the same time, prayer is our responsibility. Prayer is a key to the kingdom of heaven. It is also the key to open God's heart and our hearts as well.

A key is not given to just anyone, only to those who are faithful and responsible. As a steward of Potiphar's family, Joseph was entrusted with the great responsibility of his master's household, which he carried out faithfully. Later Joseph became the prime minister of Egypt and was entrusted with responsibility for the whole country.

The key of the kingdom of heaven is now given to each of us as God's children. We must be responsible to handle such a valuable trust.

Jesus said to Peter, "I will give you the keys of the kingdom of heaven; whatever you bind on earth will be bound in heaven, and whatever you loose on earth will be loosed in heaven" (Matthew 16:19). The keys of the kingdom of heaven are appropriated first from the earth. Whatever we bind on earth will be bound in heaven, and whatever we loose on earth will be loosed in heaven. Later, Jesus explains the relationship between the keys of the kingdom of heaven and binding, and connects it to prayer. "Again, truly I tell you that if two of you on earth agree about anything they ask for, it will be done for them by my Father in heaven" (Matthew 18:19). If we take a close look at the context of the text, the keys of the kingdom of heaven have to do with prayer and are used by us on earth.

Salvation belongs to God. He begins and ends it. But prayer and evangelism are tasks that we carry out by the power and authority of the Holy Spirit. They must begin on earth. If we read carefully the statement that Jesus made in John 1:51, the angels of God are ascending and descending on the Son of Man. Ascending is first, and then descending; not the other way around. I don't want to make a big issue about the order here, but we can find a certain pattern from it: prayer on earth first, then the angels ascend to heaven with the prayer, and then descend from heaven with the answers to the prayers.

In the book of Daniel, we see the angel Gabriel descend to earth as a response from heaven when Daniel prayed. Prayer is mystery. When we pray, there are many amazing spiritual things happening. God listens when we pray, and he moves his angels to answer our prayers. He moves people and creates the environment. God moves the whole universe.

Our prayers are a part of spiritual warfare. When we pray, Satan is getting weak. John Bunyun said, "Pray often, for prayer is a shield to the soul, a sacrifice to God, and a scourge for Satan." When we pray, we are, in fact, scourging Satan. Satan trembles at even the weakest saint who gets down on bended knees to pray.

When we pray, the power of the Holy Spirit comes upon us. When we pray humbly, God heals our land (2 Chronicles 7:14). There is nothing more mystical than prayer. Prayer is the way to our God, and a way of communication with God. It is an intimate fellowship with God.

Our living God is the God of prayer. Jesus, who was raised from death to life, is praying for us (Romans 8:34; Hebrews 7:25). Even the Holy Spirit is praying: "The Spirit helps us in our weakness" and "intercedes for us through wordless groans" (Romans 8:26).

Charles Spurgeon said, "Prayer is a golden key." E. M. Bounds also said that prayer is the key to opening God's great treasure storage. R. A. Torrey said, "Prayer is the key that unlocks all the storehouses of God's infinite grace and power." Let's give thanks to God for giving us the keys of the kingdom of heaven. Let us come before our God with the keys and pray with gratitude. God has entrusted the heavenly keys to us, so let's use them!

God does not need people searching for better methods but people on their knees in prayer. Let us not be in such a hurry that we cannot take the necessary time to pray. More than anything else, let us offer the prayer of thanksgiving, the prayer so important that Meister Eckart said, "If the only prayer you ever say in your entire life is thank you, it will be enough."

# 34

# The Gift Hidden in Difficulties

*T*rials are difficult and painful, never easy to endure. But in order to be thankful for our trials, we should study them. We must learn what they mean and what roles they play in our lives. More than anything else, we need to recognize the benefits of trials; they are often God's gifts. Of course, they are gifts we don't often want or like, but once we see their value we cannot reject these presents from God.

Trials are like a hot melting pot where we are broken, melted and cleansed. We are tested, but our true selves are allowed to emerge when we endure, strengthened by the process.

Trials can shake us, but it is during hard times that we send our roots deep to God. Roots don't grow deep in a comfortable environment where water is plentiful and the gentle breeze blows. It's during famines and forest fires that trees send their roots deep into the ground. Those trees that survive difficult seasons are often the ones that have already endured tough times.

There once was a tree pulled up by its roots in a storm. It

was floating in a river when it met a willow tree and asked, "Why were you not pulled up by the strong winds?" The willow tree answered, "I bow down when the winds are too strong." It is the flexible trees that can endure strong winds. They know how to humble themselves.

One who has passed the test and overcome the trials becomes stronger, but real strength comes from flexibility. There is power in adjustment and being soft. A person who overcomes trials well is like a flexible tree, so flexibility is true power.

Trials add value to us. The process of making dried pollock, a fish commonly found in the northern Pacific, is a good example of this. Pollock freezes during the winter to become dried pollock, but it is the cold winter weather that makes pollock into a good-quality dried pollock. Regular pollocks or just frozen pollocks are not expensive, but well-dried pollocks produced by several winter freezings are uncommon and therefore quite valuable. It is the trial that adds value to the pollock.

Likewise, trials add value to the people who go through them. Read the Bible and you will find that God's beloved people have always been tested. But as they went through trials, they grew in wisdom, maturity, humility, kindness, flexibility and holiness. Through their trials, they came forth as gold.

God can use those who have endured and overcome their trials. But in order to endure, we must accept our trials. If we are able to face difficulties without blaming others or complaining, we will grow and be given the gift of wisdom.

There is a shallow wisdom that makes us discern and diagnose incorrectly. But real wisdom is circumspection, and circumspection requires reflection and awareness. That kind of wisdom is a gift to those who overcome trials.

So we can give thanks for our trials. I still must admit that there were many days I was deeply hurt by the difficulties I faced, but those trials cleansed my spirit and made me send my roots deeply to God. God's amazing gifts were hidden in my trials, so I am thankful for hard times.

# 35

# The Love of the Cross

*G*od loved us, so he chose the cross to sacrifice his only Son. Love is sacrifice, and the width and depth of love is defined by the sacrifice. Love hurts, aches and causes the heart to pound, but it is a holy pounding. To love is to give oneself up for the object of that love.

Love hurts, but it does so willingly and joyfully. It experiences life uniquely: hurting yet joyful, painful yet pleasant. Love touches our hearts because of sacrifice; we are moved to love others when we are loved. Love leaves a mark on our souls, for we can experience love to the depths of our being. We risk when we love, becoming weak and vulnerable before the ones we love.

God made himself vulnerable on the cross because of his love for us, but love is strong. That's the paradox. Love is the only reason God can ever be said to be vulnerable. We risk when we love, yet love is strong because it risks.

The cross is where God's love is revealed, the love that

prompted the gift of his Son. To receive God's grace is to receive his love. This love has the power to change and renew people and to lift the fallen.

The love of the cross is the love of forgiveness. When Jesus washed the feet of his disciples, he knew that everyone would leave him before his crucifixion. He knew that Judas Iscariot would betray him and that Peter would deny him three times. Usually those who ask for forgiveness are compelled to kneel down, but in this case the one who forgave knelt down. Jesus knelt down to serve his disciples, inviting them to receive his forgiveness.

The most severe temptation is toward bitterness and revenge. But forgiveness leads to true freedom for those who have been hurt.

One of the greatest inventions in human history is the eraser, since it erases mistakes. The cross erases our sins. God's love is the eraser that deletes the documents where our sins were recorded, allowing us to start over.

The love of the cross is love that adds value, but our sin degrades us and diminishes our potential. We lose our position and influence due to our sin. Sin makes the beautiful ugly, but the love of God bestowed on the cross forgives sinners and transforms them into his righteous ones. His love takes all our sins and imputes us with his righteousness.

When Ruth was loved by Boaz, her value and position changed. Love is transformational. But it matters who loves us. When we are loved by God, everything about us changes. We become the righteous bride of Jesus. We are no longer children of wrath but children of God. This transformation makes us heirs of God's kingdom.

We are now people indwelt by the Holy Spirit, being transformed by God's love. Let us give thanks for the love of the cross. And let us love one another with the same kind of love we have received from God.

# 36

# The Cross and the Resurrection

*W*hen we celebrate the resurrection of Jesus Christ, we are celebrating not only the resurrection but also the crucifixion. The cross should not be forgotten because of the joy of resurrection. God chose the cross to save us and to reveal his love for us (Romans 5:8).

The cross represents suffering and descent, but the resurrection is glory and ascent, and the fruit of the resurrection is the result of the seeds of suffering. We can learn God's order, sovereignty, wisdom and power through this pairing of Good Friday and Easter morning.

From them we gain the wisdom that pain and pleasure can coexist. Life is like two intersecting lines that consist of the latitude of difficult things and the longitude of pleasant things. Often in the ups and downs of life, what seemed like good things may turn out to be bad while what seemed bad may turn out to be good. Who would have thought that dying on the cross would be a glorious thing? Who would have thought that Jesus' wounds would bring glory to God?

We learn the wisdom of patience from the crucifixion and resurrection. The waiting is important. We can't skip those dark days between the cross and the glory. Even if we long for spring because of the harsh winter, we still have no choice but to wait. And spring always comes in its time. We cannot force things to be done before their time. Our personal agendas get in the way; we rush and make mistakes. But the wise know that sometimes all we can do is wait.

We also learn the wisdom of preservation from the cross and the resurrection. In order to bear the fruit of resurrection, Jesus saved his strength on the cross. During the winter season, plants save their energy for the spring when they will sprout and bloom. During summer, nature endures the hot weather and sends roots deeply into the earth in order to bear fruit in the coming autumn season.

Those who are in a season of pain must remember that resurrection comes in due time. Winter will end and spring will come. But we must remember that there is a cross in the resurrection.

With God's touch, the rough-hewn cross is transformed into the glorious cross. A wounding cross becomes a healing cross. That's why Jesus could commit his spirit into his Father's hands (Luke 23:46).

Let us commit our lives into God's hands. Let us give thanks to God our Father for placing the resurrection in the cross and the cross in the resurrection.

# 37

# Beauty

*S*pring is beautiful. In its radiance it brings forth leaves, flowers and fruit after a long and cold winter season. Take a moment and feel this beauty as the excellent work of God. God's work in nature is simply amazing, and he shares this masterpiece with everyone! Take a moment to consider the indescribable beauty and variety of colors, scents and shapes. Experience the depth of joy of his work, which springs up and brings us refreshment.

Our observations of beauty are dependent on light. Colors change as the light changes, and without light we cannot see beauty. But God is the light that makes all things beautiful and alive. Light chases away darkness and destroys ignorance. That's why one Korean scholar said that the antonym of beauty is not "ugliness" but "ignorance." The depth of beauty is the depth of knowing.

Where does knowing come from? Love. We know when we love. We understand when we love. When we love, we see the beauty that was previously hidden from us. Think of the pregnant woman: in the classic sense she may not be considered beautiful. But no one ever thinks a pregnant woman is ugly. Why? It is because we know that a precious life is growing inside of her, which makes us appreciate her true beauty.

When we are in love, we become beautiful. In the novel *Japseolpoom*, author Sang-Ryung Park insists that the word *beauty* shares the same meaning with *heart aching*. Thus, to love is to ache, and without heartbreak one cannot love.

Jesus was wounded on the cross because of his love, but the beauty of life was the result. The ugliness of the cross was transformed into something beautiful because of his love. Paul received this love, set his mind on Jesus and came to love the cross.

True beauty begins from within our hearts. Blessed are those who can see, feel and admire beauty, for they will have a rich heart. True riches come from the inner self and are only experienced by a heart that can see true beauty.

If we hurry, we miss most of the beauty of life, so we need to slow down and even stop at times. Only when we enjoy that slowness can we experience beauty. For this reason, God often reveals true beauty to us when we go through the most difficult of times, allowing us to see things we were unable to see before. A season of darkness makes the light all the more precious to us. We come to appreciate the life we have.

Part of living a spiritual life is learning to slow down and stop. That's why spiritual formation is God's favor on us. Take a moment to pause, to look at flowers or buds on the trees. Hold tightly to a child's hand and share a radiant smile. Be thankful for the grace of our Lord that enables us to see beauty.

# 38

# A Mother's Love

*A* mother's love is sacrificial. Children start hurting their mothers from the moment they are born, and mothers bear the wounds of childbirth. They literally shed their blood to bring new life. A mother cannot turn her back on her child, for whom she suffered much. A mother and child are always one and are connected for eternity.

A mother's bosom is a lifeline for her child, a resting place. Mothers protect their children with unshakable courage. That's why we miss our mothers and cry when we think of their love.

A mother has great influence over her children. When I was young, my mother took in many poor country girls and taught them how to sew. Though she was also poor, she had great dignity and pursued this endeavor with professionalism and excellence. By watching my mother, I learned how to help others grow and discovered that there is no shame in poverty.

Although my mother was not well-educated, she was a philosopher of life and an excellent counselor. Sometimes when I was young, I would pretend to be asleep as I listened to my mom counseling other women from our village. That was how I learned about life, human nature and suffering. From my mother, I learned concern for others and how to comfort those who grieve.

My mother lived a difficult life, and her wounds allowed her to counsel well. She understood how humans are complicated by immaturities and sorrows, and she offered comfort. My mother's influence is heard in the words of my sermons and writings.

When I was in the military service, my mother wrote me a letter every week to encourage and comfort me. She also challenged me to not fall to temptations. Her letters were written with tears, prayers and the emotions of a deep heart. Sometimes she wrote to me as a friend on a difficult journey, and sometimes as her son. I learned that the best writing doesn't come from the head but from the heart. Her letters taught me how to communicate heart to heart.

My mother raised her children in prayer. While I served in the military, she literally slept at church two-thirds of the time to pray for me. Later someone told me that she often went up to a mountain to pray for me through an entire day, rain or shine. I now know that my mother's prayers were accumulated and reached the throne of God, moving his heart. Her prayers for me are treasures that have made me who I am today.

My mother taught me to be honest and punished me harshly every time I lied. I learned the value of honesty from those childhood experiences.

She also taught me to be humble, encouraging me when I faced difficult situations by saying, "If there is a hard time, there must be a good time in return." She warned me not to be too excited or become arrogant when I experienced blessings and victories.

I regret that I haven't always lived according to my mother's teachings. But each year on Mother's Day I think on her grace and love and quietly whisper, "Thanks, Mom. I love you."

# 39

# Mystery

*W*hen we say that something is mysterious, we mean it is something we might experience but not fully understand. A mystery can transcend the world of our five senses. In this way the spiritual world is a world of mystery. It is delicate and deep and mellow, and somewhat beyond our comprehension.

Our God himself is a mystery. He is not an object of our cognition but of our faith. He is not to be fully understood but to be trusted and followed. We shouldn't try to comprehend everything about God. True wisdom is to accept God's mystery as it is. It is for this reason Paul said, "Oh, the depth of the riches of the wisdom and knowledge of God! How unsearchable his judgments, and his paths beyond tracing out!" (Romans 11:33).

Scientists have tried to analyze the mystery of nature, the cosmos and even life itself. But no scientist can comprehend the mystery of God. Albert Einstein said, "The most beautiful thing we can experience is the mysterious. It is the source of all true art and all science. He to whom this emotion is a stranger, who can no longer pause to wonder and stand rapt in awe, is as good as dead: his eyes are closed." A true scientist stands in awe of God.

We can be grateful for God's mystery, since this leads us to wonder. True richness marvels at the amazing works of God. In *The Gospel of Suffering*, Søren Kierkegaard tells the parable of a wealthy man who rides comfortably and securely in his carriage on a dark night. But because he lights his lamp, he misses the magnificent display of stars across the sky that is so plainly enjoyed by the peasant driving the carriage. We view all things through the technology that science has created, but we are losing our wonder of God's world. What a tragedy!

So we need to recover a sensitivity to wonder. When spring comes, flowers bloom and butterflies appear. I marvel at the mystery of God's creation. The color, detail and movement of a tiger butterfly astound me. Who else could create such a masterpiece but God?

What great thing has humanity ever created of its own accord? I am not saying that everything made by humans is bad, but the reality is that even though we are captivated by so many human creations, they ultimately take away our happiness. Nuclear bombs and nuclear power plants make us live in fear. The internet and modern technology have created a "quickly, quickly" culture. We have lost an appreciation for waiting. Patience, self-control and love for others seem to be rare commodities these days.

In *Man Is Not Alone*, Abraham Joshua Heschel insists that ingratitude is the reason for modern society's unharmonized status. Our ingratitude is due to our lack of wonder. As we lose our sensitivity to wonder, we have become desensitized even to God's amazing grace. A life that can't feel wonder is a sad life indeed.

We need to recover our faith to accept the mystery. We need to restore our sensitivity to wonder. But our sensitivity can only be restored through spiritual training.

Our job is to give thanks to the Lord, who is a mystery. Let us know wonder and gratitude for his marvelous and mysterious works. This is our only hope for inner joy in this world.

# 40

# Good Books

*M*y life has been shaped by a series of good encounters with God and good books. In fact, God has used good books to help me grow and mature. So these encounters with good books are not mere coincidences but divine appointments.

It has been said that we are what we eat. Since books are food for the soul, I think we are what we read. Just as our physical condition can change when we change what we eat, our attitudes change when we change what we read. Good books are a pathway to good language, good thinking and a good attitude.

The Chinese word *tao* (道) means "way." It can also mean "open." When we open books, pathways are opened to us. Our hearts are opened. Our lives, our futures and our eternities are opened. When we read, we find otherwise hidden paths.

I love seeing an author's spirit and heart in a book because it allows me to dialogue with the author while I read. A book is a divine instrument that helps me meet good people regardless of time and space.

Good books are treasures, but the Book of books is the Bible. I find the way as I read the Bible. I meet Jesus and gain new life as I read Scripture. When we read the Word of life, God's life flows into us; our souls are healed, our spirits strengthened, and we are filled abundantly.

But we should also read good books—the classics—along with the Bible. These books contain unchanging truth and answer many of life's problems. They contain common language that transcends time, words such as *suffering, pain, dreams, faith, hope* and *love*. We can gain inspiration, transcendent knowledge and wisdom from good books.

Learning brings about change as ideas stimulate and challenge us, and books are our learning tools. Changes occur when there is confrontation between the existing knowledge and new knowledge. By reading, we come to know new things and can be reacquainted with things we once knew but had forgotten. Books can open our eyes, helping us to consider what we already know and what we don't yet know. We can be enlightened by what we read.

God loves books. In fact, books are God's idea. God let Moses write a part of the Bible. He commanded Joshua to read and meditate on the Scripture. Even Jesus regularly read the Scripture. Toward the end of his life in a Roman prison, the apostle Paul asked Timothy to "bring the books" to him. Those books were a great treasure to the lonely Paul.

Books can become our friends when we feel lonely. Books give everything they have for those who love them. They expose us to beautiful ideals, reform and renew the way we think, cause a revolution of understanding, give us wisdom and teach us the art of love.

The hopeful future belongs to readers. So many of the

world's great leaders were prolific readers. The treasures of humanity are hidden in great books. Remember that there are ways in books, so book readers have spiritual wealth.

Even now God is working through good books. More than anything else he is working through the Book of books. Let us read good books and, more than anything, read the Bible. Return to God who speaks through the Scripture, for this is how we grow in maturity and usefulness for God's kingdom.

# 41

## An Art of Life

*G*iving thanks is more than an important life skill; it's an art. Grateful people live the lives of artists, who create things. Human creativity is not about creating something out of nothing (that's *God's* specialty) but finding hidden beauty and revealing it. An artist sees something in an abandoned piece of marble that no one else sees. The creative act is making that masterpiece visible to others.

Artists see things differently. Michelangelo's *David* is an amazing example of this. The block of marble used for the sculpture had already been worked on and abandoned fifty years earlier by Agostino de Duccio. Michelangelo saw the completed David inside that useless piece of marble. All he had to do was set the hidden David free.

Art and gratitude are both about revelation. Art reveals hidden beauty, and gratitude reveals reasons to be thankful, even in circumstances that block the view of others. In this way, gratitude reveals the inner beauty of people.

Great artists are able to turn something looked down on

into something precious. It is the ability to reveal love and beauty from the lives of isolated people. I am not suggesting they neglect reality. In fact, if we move people's hearts by honestly embracing people's pain and revealing their stories, we are artists. Feeling the pain and suffering that most would rather avoid and yet revealing their delight, worth and beauty is art.

Consider the great masterpieces. Their primary themes are suffering, pain and hurt, yet they have transformed difficulty into beauty.

An artist makes a beautiful masterpiece through control and discipline. A sculptor reveals beauty by cutting and shaving away. Actors prepare for and film movies, but the movie is edited down to create something that touches our hearts.

Writers discover that it is more difficult to write a short and simple sentence than a long one. In fact, writing a simple sentence is not easy at all. To keep only the necessary words and let others go is the art of language. This is why poets are so impressive—they are able to move people's hearts with limited words.

Gratitude is an art. The language of gratitude is short and simple. The words are well controlled, but they touch people's hearts. When we give thanks, few words are needed. There will certainly be moments we feel sorrowful or hurt by injustices we suffer, and there are appropriate times and places to express our hurt to the proper people. But it's not wise to express all our feelings without control, and complaining does not resolve our situation. The art of gratitude is to cut the useless words away and keep only what is helpful.

Gratitude involves finding and expressing what we are thankful for. We should examine ourselves to see how we feel and what happens to us when we give thanks. Pay attention to how relationships are improved and how the hearts of others are touched through gratitude. These insights can bring us deeper into the world of gratitude. Let us all become artists of gratitude, who can give thanks in all circumstances.

# 42

# The Joy of Playing

*J*ust as parents are pleased by their children's pleasure, God is pleased when we know pleasure. Remember, God is our loving Father, and we are his children; play is a gift from him. We often use play as a verb: we play sports, we play musical instruments, we play games, and so on. Some cultures, such as Korean, have a negative connotation of play. That connotation has more to do with how we play and who we play with. But as long as our play is not about the pleasure of sin, play is a wonderful gift and even a divine, creative art.

We can learn about pleasure by observing children at play. They are able to forget about their surroundings and immerse themselves in play. There is an invisible rhythm and tempo to their play, filled with various facial expressions, hand gestures and foot actions. Never seeming to tire from play, their creativity actually invigorates them.

We enjoyed playing when we were young, but we seemed to have forgotten how to play as we have grown older. We are very serious. No laughter. No smiles. Our work is a curse. Of course, it is important to be serious, but if anything is too serious for too long then it becomes a heavy burden. We miss out on the abundant life when we live that way.

To play is to pursue simple and genuine pleasure. A key to this is expecting less and enjoying more. If we can enjoy work the way children enjoy play, then we will know joy.

Play helps us discover the hidden potential within, and the pleasure of play helps us achieve excellence. Excellence comes from repetition, and in order to repeat something over and over, it must be fun. Proficiency comes from practice, and practice comes from the heart of play. Once we know the joy of jogging, we want to run more. Whether it is music, art, reading, prayer or meditation, when the experience brings pleasure, then we want to do more. Excellence and enjoyment go together. So Confucius, an ancient Chinese philosopher, said, "Better than to know something is to like it. Better than to like something is to enjoy it."

In order to recover pleasure we need to learn again how to play. In *Playing and Reality*, English pediatrician and psychoanalyst Donald Winnicott insists that therapists "enable the patient to become able to play." A person unable to play is locked in, but play sets us free. We need to restore our childlike attitudes, to cultivate them, to dance, sing and play as though no one else is around. Be a child before God and enjoy his presence.

There is a close relationship between creativity and play. Carl Jung said, "The creation of something new is not accomplished by the intellect but by the play instinct acting from inner necessity. The creative mind plays with the objects it loves." Play helps us discover the hidden potential deep within us.

God knows how difficult our lives are, how heavy our burdens and how hurtful our wounds. That's why he gave us the gift of play. As Eugene Peterson says, "Christ plays in ten thousand places," in creation, history and community. Creation is a fruit of divine play, so when we play we become more like our Father.

Satan hates joy, so he tempts us to pursue the counterfeit pleasures of sin. But our God is the God of joy and pleasure, and righteous play is his gift to us. We can give thanks to him for this precious gift. Now it is our job to use the gift well.

# 43

## Strange Places

*W*e learn something that can't be learned from books when we travel. In *Travel Off the Map*, writer and humanitarian Bi-ya Han refers to travel as "school on the street." Because I am very weak, traveling is always a challenge for me. So it is a mystery to me how I gain new strength each time I return from a trip. I learn something new every time. As Lance Morrow reminds us, "People travel because it teaches them things they could learn no other way."

Travel can open our eyes to discover new things, to see things we haven't seen before and feel things we've never felt. Marcel Proust said in *Remembrance of Things Past*, "The real voyage of discovery consists not in seeking new landscapes, but in having new eyes." When we travel, we develop new eyes.

As we travel, we encounter the God who works in history and learn his ways. I once had the opportunity to travel to Turkey, where 98 percent of the population is Muslim. These followers of Islam live near their mosques and pray to Allah five times a day. Even though their faith teaches them to be kind to strangers, it is a very difficult environment for missionaries to share the gospel.

But Turkey is significant to Christians. The apostle Paul came from Tarsus, and the first Gentile church was in Antioch. Cappadocia has underground hiding places where persecuted Christians found safety under Roman rule.

I traveled to the sites of the seven churches and the places where Paul ministered. Turkey is filled with places sacred to Christianity, but now it is a mission field where very few Christians live. During my time in Turkey, I prayed for the souls there more than ever before. Travel can make us pray.

Travel also allows us to start new relationships. During my time in Turkey, I made new relationships with new people and began a new relationship with the nation. Turkey became an unforgettable land and a focal point for my prayers.

Many Christians go on mission trips every summer. They travel to a strange place to share the gospel, to pray and to share God's love with local people. But another reason to go on a mission trip is to start a new relationship with a new place.

Sometimes we plan a trip hoping to change someone, but instead we return home to find that we were changed. We think we can be a blessing to others, but the blessing falls on us, and such blessings fill us with gratitude.

# 44

# Silence

*I*n *Invitation to Love,* Thomas Keating writes, "Silence is God's first language; everything else is a poor translation." There is a weight and depth to silence because it is God's language. Words that emerge from silence have power.

Silence and solitude go hand in hand. Solitude is the doorway to silence. Without solitude, quietness is difficult to achieve.

The peace of our hearts comes from silence. When a lake is calm, you can see a reflection of the sky on its surface. But on a turbulent lake, the sky cannot be seen. In the same way, when the mind is calm, it can reflect heavenly inspiration, but the shaking heart cannot feel heavenly inspiration.

People like depth. They pursue deep understanding, deep taste and deep relationships. The world of silence is a deep world, but for some reason many of us are afraid of entering in. Those who have yet to experience the blessing of silence are vulnerable to the attacks of fear when they decide not to speak for a day.

Silence is not easy. Have you ever tried to be silent when

you were insulted? Can you keep silence when you are misunderstood? How about when you are angry? When Jesus
was mocked and insulted, he remained silent.

Silence is born of self-control. To take control of oneself is
an art, since it requires doing what one *must* do and not what
one *prefers* to do. But self-control brings freedom.

Through silence we discern what we should and should not
say. Depending on context, the very same words can bring
forth different results. But we can learn to speak the proper
words in the proper time. It is written in the Bible, "A person
finds joy in giving an apt reply—and how good is a timely
word!" (Proverbs 15:23). Language that comes through silence
has a heartbeat, but language without silence has no power.
This is why Pythagoras said, "It is better wither to be silent, or
to say things of more value than silence. Sooner throw a pearl
at hazard than an idle or useless word; and do not say a little
in many words, but a great deal in a few."

We care for the inner flame through silence. When we
speak too much, the flame fades and our hearts grow cold. A
cold heart becomes hardened, and this produces stub-
bornness; that heart chases away flexibility, allowing obduracy
room to settle down. But the human heart is meant to be
warm and soft, since that is how life is sustained. When we
keep silent, we maintain that kind of heart. Warm words flow
from a warm heart. Soft language comes from a soft heart.
But the flame of the Holy Spirit can be quenched when we talk
too much.

Just as we learn language, we need to exercise and practice
silence every day. When we practice silence, it does not mean
that we should not speak at all but that we should be disci-
plined to only speak the truth in love.

God created the universe with words. He teaches us with his words, heals us and comforts us, touches and changes us, creates new history, and gives us hope through his words. The reason God's words have such power is that they come from deep silence.

When our words emerge from deep silence, they can touch people's hearts. Let us limit our speaking and have more times of silence. If we can be silent, then we will hear more of God's voice and learn to listen to others. We can be thankful for God's gift of silence.

# 45

# A Holy Touch

*W*e live in a generation full of connection but short of touch. As soon as we open our eyes in the morning, we connect to the internet, gathering information for our day. But information alone is not enough. We are living creatures who need the warmth of touch. Touch is God's gift, and once we know its meaning our lives can be richer.

In modern society, many people suffer from what I call touching deficiency syndrome (TDS). TDS makes people lonely; our emotions can become as dry as an empty well. But TDS can be cured by holy touch.

We need a balance of physical, emotional and spiritual touch. All three are essential because we consist of body, mind and soul. Among the five senses, touch is our most acute. It starts from the moment of conception; contact receptors develop before visual or audio senses. Because of the experience in the mother's womb, humans long to be touched for the rest of their lives.

Touch is a mediating method of love; it is a language we use to share and express our love. In *Emile*, Jean-Jacques Rousseau writes, "To live is not to breathe but to act. It is to make use of our organs, our senses, our faculties, of all the parts of ourselves which give us the sentiment of our existence. The man who has lived the most is not he who has counted the most years but he who has most felt life." To live is so much more than to breathe. To live is to love and to feel. And our love is communicated through touch.

The warmth of love is transferred through touch. Touch renews us, strengthening and moving our hearts. Unfortunately, not all touching is good. Some touch can be annoying or even sinful. Those who suffer from TDS can easily fall into inappropriate touching. We must be cautious since sinful touch can bring serious consequences.

Touch has various forms. Words of encouragement and thanksgiving bring a warm touch. Music has the power to touch and heal our souls. Through worship and the Word of God, we are connected to him and his kingdom, which is how we are touched by him.

God's holy and divine touch can heal us. When Jesus healed the sick, he often touched them. The laying on of hands invokes God's power of healing; this kind of touch heals not only the body but also the heart.

God allows us to be filled with the Spirit through touch. When Moses laid hands on Joshua, he was filled with the spirit of wisdom (Deuteronomy 34:9). Because God is almighty, he pours out his Spirit on his people.

We can become filled by holy touch; it sanctifies us. The turning point of my life began through the touch of Jesus. Through it I received new life and have been transformed by his continuing fellowship. Jesus healed me from TDS. That touch was a holy touch, and for this I am forever thankful.

# 46

# Contentment

*G*ratitude comes from self-contentment. To be self-content is to be without need. It's not the environment or circumstances of life that make people miserable but the inability to control desire. Happiness is not about satisfying desires but controlling them; the happiest people are those who are self-content.

Our true wealth lies in the attitude of our hearts. Socrates said, "He is richest who is content with the least, for contentment is the wealth of nature." Human happiness does not depend on possessions but on our heart's attitude and beautiful relationships. To be spiritually rich is to be truly rich.

When we are truly content, others have no power to make us unhappy. In the same way, no amount of material wealth can produce true contentment. Happiness comes from the habit of self-contentment.

Spiritual discipline is a training that cultivates our inner world. Self-contentment is not natural, so we train for it through serious spiritual discipline, knowing that true riches come from a well-tended inner world.

The apostle Paul knew how to be self-content. He rejoiced over and over again, even in prison, because he had learned to be content: "I am not saying this because I am in need, for I have learned to be content whatever the circumstances. I know what it is to be in need, and I know what it is to have plenty. I have learned the secret of being content in any and every situation, whether well fed or hungry, whether living in plenty or in want" (Philippians 4:11-12).

Putting what we learn into practice is called *training*. We need this practice so that we neither fall before prosperity nor become servile before poverty. In *Prayer: What Difference Does It Make?* Philip Yancey records a dialogue between a monk and a spiritual seeker in a monastery. As the monk shows the seeker to his room, the monk says, "I hope your stay is a blessed one. If you need anything, just let us know and we'll teach you how to live without it."

In order to be self-content, we must learn how to adjust and transcend our circumstances, rejoicing regardless of the environment. But we can only do this when we find our contentment in Christ Jesus. In *The Weight of Glory*, C. S. Lewis sums it up like this: "He who has God and everything else has no more than he who has God only."

Self-contentment contributes to godliness, as Paul taught his spiritual son, Timothy: "But godliness with contentment is great gain" (1 Timothy 6:6).

The wise know what they already have and have learned to enjoy it. We search far and wide for happiness when contentment is all around. What makes us rich is our faith in Jesus; the root of self-contentment is trusting him for everything.

The Christian's life goal should not be earning and maintaining possessions. Those who have faith in Jesus as their Lord and Savior know that he is their only source of contentment for eternity. Let us train ourselves for contentment and experience the riches of heaven every day.

# 47

# Tears

*A* hardened heart cannot give thanks to the Lord. Such a heart is stubborn, which leads to wickedness. Repentance softens the hard heart, and repentance often involves tears. Tears may come from our eyes, but they always wet our hearts.

Wounds must be dealt with carefully. If not, they become callouses and scars. This is especially true of the wounds to our hearts. If not cared for properly, those wounds can scar, shutting down the gates of our hearts and affecting all our relationships.

Our hearts can't function well unless they are open. Closed hearts bring tragedy, so do not hold back tears. Tears are like a balm that cures wounds and washes away the pain of the soul. They have a healing power to help resolve our emotional anger and massage our feelings. Emotional pain should be transformed into holy energy. Tears do that for us. God created tears for a purpose—even Jesus wept.

Like holy water washing the windows of the soul, tears

spring from our deepest parts. Only when the eyes of the soul are clean can we see God and others properly. In the poem "Tears and Laughter," Kahlil Gibran expresses gratitude for tears, which "purify my heart and reveal to me the secret of life and its mystery." With tears comes new understanding for people and for life.

The prayer that comes through tears moves the heart of God and touches the heart of people. When Hezekiah was about to die, he prayed and wept. When God spoke to him through Isaiah, he said, "I have heard your prayers and seen your tears" (Isaiah 38:5). God added fifteen years to Hezekiah's life.

Tears are a language that reveals truth without words. Babies announce their birth with a cry and communicate with their mothers through tears. Only later do babies learn to communicate through smiles and then words. Tears transcend language, culture and ethnicity. Honest tears speak louder than words. They express our gratitude and love, and they communicate inexpressible wonder. Tears even provide comfort to others in pain.

Jesus taught, "Blessed are those who mourn, for they will be comforted" (Matthew 5:4). God's comfort of peace comes after streaming tears, so let us not be afraid of crying. Our hearts are softened and new strength is gained through the shedding of tears. We can be healed or even change our direction through repentance with sincere tears. And when we cry, we can understand each other. Crying can unclog the channels of our emotions.

Tears are treasures. Let us be grateful for God's precious gift of tears.

# 48

# The Comma

*A* period and comma look very similar, but there is a clear difference between them, a difference not to be taken lightly. We may mistake a comma for a period if we don't pay close attention to the difference.

A rest in music is very important. A rest mark on a musical chart gives the musician a chance to breathe. Without those rests, the music becomes noise.

In the same way, God is the composer of our lives. He knows where we should rest, and that is where he places the comma. He may use failures, illnesses, difficulties, conflicts or obstacles, but one way or another God gets us to rest.

When God puts a comma in our lives, we have no choice but to take a break during our failures, defeats and frustrations. It's a temporary stop sign to shift direction or recharge ourselves. We might need to stop to love other people or to read and write. Just as we rest in the night and work in the day, temporary stops provide a rhythm to life.

At the same time, we must remember that a comma is not

a period; it is not an end. While we rest, we need to prepare for the next step of life's long journey. It is an opportunity to stop and reflect or check our direction. Failures stop us temporarily, but they must not be eternal stops. We should not give up.

One should not be arrogant in success, since no success lasts forever. But neither does failure need to have the final word in our lives. So we need to balance our thinking daily. We can do this tuning of our minds through the spiritual disciplines, such as morning devotions or meditation on the Word of God.

God puts commas in my life from time to time. Sometimes they arrive in the form of failure, frustration or depression. At times I have mistaken a comma for a period, leading to discouragement and disappointment. But as I look back, those commas provided an opportunity for reflection and healing. God renewed me during those times, making me see things I couldn't have seen otherwise and understand things that I had not understood before.

God has led me to a deeper world that I would not have entered without his commas. For those who are taking a break after hitting a huge wall, take courage! Don't put a period where God has put a comma. Take this temporary rest time as a springboard for a new season of life. God is a good God who knows when we need rest.

# 49

# Holy Darkness

*A* mong many kinds of darkness, there is something that I call holy darkness. Nobody likes darkness. But not all darkness is bad. In fact, we were all born through darkness. A mother's womb is dark. That's where we developed and grew before birth. Darkness was there before creation. In the beginning, when God created the universe, what the Holy Spirit embraced was "formless and empty, [and] darkness was over the surface of the deep" (Genesis 1:2). Before God created light, there was deep darkness.

When I was reading Isaiah 45:3, "I will give you the treasures of darkness, riches stored in secret places, so that you may know that I am the LORD, the God of Israel, who summons you by name" (NIV 1984), I could not understand what it meant. Why would God put treasures in darkness? The Genesis story helped me understand. Before creating a new thing, God let it go through darkness first. Author Sue Monk Kidd went through a dark period of time, chronicled in her memoir *When the Heart Waits*, but as she went through those difficult days she came to understand it as "a *holy* dark."

To incubate means to create the conditions necessary for development. What were those conditions, I wondered? Then it hit me: *darkness.* Everything incubates in darkness. And I know that the darkness in which I found myself was a holy darkness. I was incubating something new. Whenever new life grows and emerges, darkness is crucial to the process. As Kidd writes, "Whether it's the caterpillar in the chrysalis, the seed in the ground, the child in the womb, or the True Self in the soul, there's always a time of waiting in the dark."

If a life is incubated in darkness, and darkness is crucial to the process of everything, we must learn to wait with expectation in the darkness. Waiting has two faces, one active and the other passive. At times we can't do anything while waiting. But amazing things happen while we wait. For example, a fetus in its mother's womb is growing tremendously while waiting to be born. A butterfly in a chrysalis is experiencing an amazing transformation, even though it is unseen. A baby chicken in an egg by a hen's bosom is growing beautifully. All these things are happening in darkness while waiting. Sometimes God takes his time to accomplish his purposes, and as a result of the wait, people think he is working too slowly. But the great things of life take time!

Through darkness, God makes us see things that we have not seen before. He helps us to see the bright future. Consider the way that God designed our eyes. We see through the black part—the iris—of the eye, not through the white part. Why did God create us to see things through the black part of the eye? It is a mystery that we see the bright future through darkness.

God allows his people to go through dark periods of life.

Joseph was thrown into a pit. He spent two years in a dark prison. Those dark years, God was preparing a stage for Joseph to demonstrate God's power and glory. While Joseph was waiting, amazing things were happening. God had Pharaoh dream a dream. In fact, that dream was not for Pharaoh, but for Joseph. David spent time in the cave of Adullam. God trained David through that time spent in darkness. David was sanctified in the dark cave and gained wisdom through dark times. God changed David from a shepherd who took care of his father's sheep to a king who would lead the Israelites. When we wait, God works.

This generation is addicted to speed. Everything seems to be about speed and quickness. Everything is in a hurry, and patience is no longer a virtue. But we must remember that our souls prefer slowness and quietness above speed and noise. Being slow doesn't mean being lazy. Slowness of soul is for listening to God's voice and seeing God's work. Slowness also allows us to taste the beauty of life. Gandhi says, "There is more to life than simply increasing its speed."

When God allows you to go through a tunnel of darkness, don't be discouraged. God allows the holy darkness for you so that he can control your life speed. Wait with gratitude in the darkness and foresee a bright future. Give God enough time so that he can work in your life. If we wait with patience, we will experience the bright future God is preparing for us.

# 50

# A Quiet Spirit

*A*lthough storms rage and waves swell, the ocean floor remains ever quiet and deeply peaceful. We might be in a small boat at sea, tossed about by powerful winds. In order to experience peace, courage is required to dive deep. The Holy Spirit shines in the place of great silence.

In order to experience quietness, we need to train ourselves to be alone and still. Most of us are afraid of isolation and silence. In *Pensées*, Blaise Pascal says, "All of humanity's problems stem from man's inability to sit quietly in a room alone." We need to learn how to embrace solitude and quiet in God's presence.

The noisy culture of this world is the consequence of anxiety and impatience. When our souls are influenced by the secular culture, we become easily shaken, feeling uneasy and insecure. Like the Israelites who fashioned a golden calf while waiting for Moses on Mount Sinai (Exodus 32), idols are the products of our fears when we cannot be still before God.

The ancient Chinese philosopher Zhuangzi once said, "To

a mind that is still, the entire universe surrenders." The wise person is one who cultivates stillness in the heart. Silent language comes from a silent heart. Silent kindness comes from a silent heart. And silent touch comes from a silent heart. In a very real sense, God's throne is at the center of our hearts. We can come to God, who dwells on the throne of our hearts, when there is silence.

Peter encourages us to cultivate our hearts, our inner selves. Instead of focusing on "outward adornment," beauty is found in the "inner self, the unfading beauty of a gentle and quiet spirit, which is of great worth in God's sight" (1 Peter 3:4). That quiet spirit comes from cultivating a quiet heart.

Our spirits like stillness. God created the heavens and the earth in stillness, and God's language is the language of stillness. In *The Enlightened Mind*, Meister Eckhart says, "God wants nothing of you but the gift of peaceful hearts." Only when we give him our peaceful hearts can God complete his mysterious and sacred word in our spirits.

Stillness starts with silence, so set apart some times of silence to give your peaceful heart to God. One of the best ways to cultivate a quiet spirit is to prohibit ourselves from the criticism of others. Putting down the uprising criticism is key to keeping a quiet spirit. Instead we can pray for those we want to criticize.

Love silence, and cultivate a quiet heart within. Undisturbed peace dwells in the silent spirit. Become an ambassador of peace by cultivating a quiet spirit and then living out that stillness you have experienced. Light this world with a smile that flows out of a quiet spirit.

# 51

# Holy Curiosity

*C*uriosity begins with interest. It means we are alert to something and may have questions. In 1841, Rev. John Todd admonished students: "Seize the moment of excited curiosity on any subject to solve your doubts:—for if you let it pass, the desire may never return; and you may remain in ignorance." Curiosity creates a desire for finding answers to our questions; we can be grateful for this holy curiosity.

The right curiosity leads us to right learning and right knowledge. Adam and Eve had the wrong kind of curiosity, which led to the fall. In *To Know as We Are Known*, Parker Palmer warns about this false curiosity:

> The sin, the error, is not our hunger for knowledge—and the way back to Paradise is not via intentional ignorance (despite some latter-day Christian claims). Adam and Eve were driven from the Garden because of the *kind* of knowledge they reached for—a knowledge that distrusted and excluded God. Their drive to know arose not from love but from curiosity and control, from the desire

to possess powers belonging to God alone. They failed to honor the fact that God knew them first, knew them in their limits as well as their potentials. In their refusal to know as they were known, they reached for a kind of knowledge that always leads to death.

Palmer emphasizes that true learning does not result from false curiosity or a desire for control. True learning must be based on love. Our questions should lead us to love God more and compel us to obey his Word.

Even though curiosity resulted in the fall of the human race, we should not condemn curiosity. It was curiosity that led to my interest in gratitude. This kind of interest is mysterious. Every time I read the Bible, the verses about thanksgiving and gratitude caught my eye. Books on gratitude grabbed my attention, and articles on gratitude touched my heart. I met people of gratitude and began to experience it myself.

To me, writing is the fruit of holy curiosity, and holy curiosity is God's favor. This divine curiosity compels us to learn and grow. It makes us more sensitive and aware, leading us to look deeper. This kind of curiosity can lead us to wisdom and excellence.

When Albert Einstein was asked about his special talent, he didn't use words such as intelligence, luck or good connections. Instead he answered with one word: curiosity. He said, "I have not special talent. I am only passionately curious."

When we become curious, we enter into a whole new world. Curiosity often leads us to new dimensions of learning, sometimes challenging us and sometimes refreshing us. Divine curiosity has the power to change us and bring us into contact with the marvelous.

Our curiosity about gratitude is a divine curiosity. William Blake said, "Gratitude is heaven itself." It is God's blessing and favor that I became curious about gratitude. This curiosity has allowed me to live with it and form a habit of gratitude. In the process, I have meditated on the God who is the source and object of my gratitude. I have tasted heaven through this experience. I am thankful for the spring of gratitude that never runs dry.

# 52

# The Glory of God

*T*he deepest gratitude is gratitude for God's glory. True worship is filled with holy flames when God's people experience his glory and come to his throne with joy. How wonderful it is to rejoice in God's glory! What a blessing it is to receive God's glory and reflect it to the world! What a glory it is to be transformed into Christlikeness as we see the face of Jesus! Isn't this the peak of spiritual formation?

The world's glory is like a flower that blooms instantly and fades just as quickly, or like a mirage appearing for an instant but ultimately proving to be an illusion. It is focused only on the life of this world, and its pursuit is vain. But God's glory lasts forever because it is the only true glory. And because it is everlasting, it can be experienced in this world and in the world to come.

The Hebrew word for glory is *kabod*, and it means "weight." God's glory is indeed weighty. It includes his excellence, his perfect works, his flawless character—goodness, mercy, compassion, forgiveness, acceptance and love—and his abundant grace.

In the Old Testament, God's glory was manifested in the tabernacle and temple. In the New Testament, God's glory is revealed through Jesus who "is the radiance of God's glory and the exact representation of his being" (Hebrews 1:3). The glory of Jesus reaches its pinnacle through the love he exhibited on the cross, restoring what was lost in the fall.

God created man and woman in his image and shined his own glory upon them, but since the fall, humanity has covered God's glory instead of revealing it. Our eyes were blinded to the glory of God, but Jesus came to open our eyes so we can see his glory and to restore God's glory in us, and with opened eyes we begin to see the glory of God that is fully present around us. With this in mind, Ralph Waldo Emerson offers us an exhortation: "Never lose an opportunity of seeing anything beautiful, for beauty is God's handwriting."

The people from Jesus' hometown didn't respect him, so they couldn't see the glory of God revealed in him. But those who see Jesus with respect will see and taste the fullness of God's glory in him. Likewise, we must see our brothers and sisters with respect in order to recognize God's glory reflected on their faces. In *The Weight of Glory*, C. S. Lewis reminds us, "There are no ordinary people."

Rejoice in God's glory. Soak in God's favor that transforms us into his likeness with "ever-increasing glory" (2 Corinthians 3:18). This is the goal of a spirituality of gratitude and the only way for us to fully experience God's glory here on earth.

# Acknowledgments

*T*his book grew out of a long season of suffering. I was going through the toughest, longest and darkest tunnel of my life, and I came to a fork in the road. I had to choose whether I would harbor bitterness toward those who had hurt me, for the rest of my life, or choose to give thanks to the Lord for everything and move on. God poured his mercy on me and led me to choose thanksgiving over blaming. And he led me to write about gratitude. I wrote about gratitude every week for a year: 52 essays.

I experienced healing and transformation as I wrote about gratitude. In fact, these essays were not originally written for other people, but for myself. Gratitude led to more gratitude. Thanksgiving overflowed as I gave thanks. Gratitude: this thanksgiving attitude seemed to clean the window of my soul. Gratitude enabled me to see the things that I had been missing. It healed the wounds that were deep within. I came to recognize that the problems were not in circumstances or other people, but within me. These writings about gratitude helped me to stand firm again so that I could start all over.

Writing a book is just like giving birth to a child. I'd like to thank Cindy Bunch, editorial director at IVP, who encouraged me to keep writing and to publish this book. Without her consistent encouragement and thoughtful consideration, this book would not have come to be. Also, many thanks also go to Dr. B. J. Jun, who translated my Korean to English in spite of his busy teaching schedule in his new position at ACTS. I would also like to thank Rev. Doug Spriggs, who smoothed Dr. Jun's English translation.

I wish to thank Tae-hyung Lee for allowing me to write about gratitude for a year for the Kookmin Daily. It is by God's grace that I have been invited to publish these essays with IVP. And I owe much to Richard Foster for his love, grace and friendship. Because of his love for me, I came to know the people of IVP and became a part of the IVP family. I want to thank him once more. Above all, my utmost thanks goes to my God, who shined upon me and gave me a heart of gratitude when I was in the darkest moment of life. Thank you, Lord!

# Other books from InterVarsity Press by Joshua Choonmin Kang

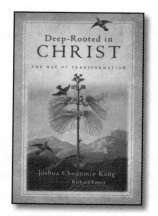

**Deep-Rooted in Christ:**
**The Way of Transformation**
978-0-8308-3511-9

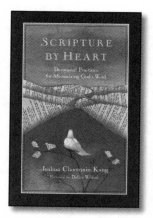

**Scripture by Heart: Devotional**
**Practices for Memorizing God's Word**
978-0-8308-3536-2